Award Winning Author

Kathleen Fuller, PH.D.

Not Your

MOTHER'S

DIET

The CURE for your EATING ISSUES

For regular updates, free tips & tools, or to subscribe to the newsletter,
visit www.notyourmothersdiet.com

www.notyourmothersdiet.com

ISBN:1-4196-8990-8
ISBN-13: 9781419689901

Visit www.booksurge.com to order additional copies.

Contents

My Spiral Work

I provide safety and hope to others. I watch them as they walk into solid walls, as I once did for three decades. The same ones over and over again, and I offer a new direction.

The 8 Essentials to Weight Loss Balance
1. Food Allergies Addressed
2. Chronic Candidiasis Addessed
3. Way too many Carbohydrates
4. Exercise
5. Corrected Hormone Imbalances
6. Brain Neurotransmitters
7. Abandoned Inner Child Healing
8. Spiritual Surrender

Look Within for Your Answers—Kathleen Fuller, PH.D.

Acknowledgments

Within every problem is a gift waiting to be discovered. I'm fortunate to have had the experience of struggling with the problem of an eating disorder in this lifetime—and experiencing the blessing of overcoming it.

Exploring eating disorders gave me more than answers about why it happens. I've discovered solutions that address and alleviate the problem at its source. As a result, I live by these spiritual truths every day. This experience has given me the impetus to share these truths and insights with others by writing this book.

So many shining stars helped me write this book, both directly and indirectly. First, I'd like to thank my pre-publication editor, Coleen Rehm. Without her knowingness, endless patience, and dedication to her profession, I could never have written this book. She is a bright shining star of God who has catapulted me into new awareness. I'd also like to thank my longtime friend, Denise Nearing for referring me to Linda Anderson who ultimately directed me to Coleen.

Many writers inspired me at the 2000 ECK Writers and Creative Arts Conference in Montreal. Thanks to Vicki Williams who graciously offered to read the first rough draft. I'd like to extend my warm gratitude to Rainbow Sally Glassburn, who gave creativity and love, and Beverly Bowles who helped me stay balanced. Many thanks go to my assistant Marty Rapert who did whatever job I needed done.

Gratitude goes to my family: first to my love, Jeff Lang who nurtured me with back rubs to help release stress from typing at night and on weekends. To my oldest daughter Danielle Crouch, who helped me enter the manuscript into the new computer. David Scarpa helped pick out and set up my new notebook computer. Thank you to my youngest daughter Shannon Crouch for her continued love notes that helped uplift me. Love and thanks also to my Mom and Dad, Sue and Weldon Fuller, and Grandma Nettie and Grandpa Frank Fuller and Grandmother Susie Matthews and Grandfather Edward Matthews for their gifts of many challenges, which have been transformed into polished diamonds in my life.

To Margo Maine, Ph.D., for her words of wisdom at EDAP's Eating Disorder Conference. Also to R.D. Longacre, Ph.D., who took time to show me that getting started is easy with an outline of my first draft at the International Hypnosis Conference in 1996. And thanks to everyone who said, "Go for it!" in response to this dream. All of you were so precious in this incredible process.

Special thanks to the DCT Team 2 Crystal & Megan for their care in loving my book in the publishing/designing process and Lee Sanderline, publishing consultant.

Special thanks to Harold Klemp who has given me spiritual support and inner guidance for many years. Without him, I wouldn't be here today.

Thank you all and I love you.

Forward

It is a pleasure to write a foreword for this well-written, easily read, and accurately presented new book *Not Your Mother's Diet—The Cure for your Eating Issues*, by Kathleen Fuller, Ph.D. The author takes a complex subject and makes it understandable. Eating issues are so startlingly multifaceted that certainly what you have heard and read in the past was one expert's approach to just a sliver of this expansive subject. Dr. Fuller not only broadens the horizons of weight problems, eating disorder issues and body image challenges to a much more eclectic view, she makes it all comprehensible.

Not Your Mother's Diet is aptly titled. My clinical experience with weight loss dieting and eating issues is that most dieters adopt an *insane* approach to achieving their goals. Insane, in that Albert Einstein defined insanity as "doing the same thing over and over again and expecting different result." How many of you have given in to the next magazine article or book or friends' advise about the "new—really works this time" diet? Isn't it about time a truly different way of looking at your diet and weight situation be explored?

For the first time in our history on earth the masses are faced with the challenges of the "abuse of abundance". Never before could the average citizen eat as much food as they wanted, 24 hours per day, 7 days per week. Even kings and queens could not do that in days of old. We must utilize new attitudes, approaches and techniques to meet these never before seen challenges.

In this self-help book we are shown how to turn these stumbling blocks into stepping stones and actually learn and grow from the experience. Dr. Fuller shares her successful, powerful and empowering tools with the reader. How refreshing to be given health, diet and eating issue tools instead of just another set of rules.

The cornucopia of creative techniques shared in *Not Your Mother's Diet* should assure the health and wellness seeker success in conquering their weight management challenges.

Dr. Fuller masterfully teaches you to use these tools to replace restricting, out-dated, non-productive premises and assumptions you unconsciously may be harboring. She encourages you to discover hidden obstacles standing between you and your greater level of health and replace those land mines with springboards.

Congratulations to Dr. Kathleen Fuller for a book that is extremely well done. *Not Your Mother's Diet* will education millions about diet, body image, eating issues and well being.

Let your liberating adventure begin. *The Cure for your Eating Issues* starts now.

Jason P. Schwartz, D.C.
Holistic Chiropractic Physician

The Journey Begins

It is a hot, steamy day in Stuart. The wind blows off the St. Lucie River. Faintly I hear the clang of sailboat masts anchored a few hundred feet off the seawall near my office. The phone rings. A woman we'll call Sherry is looking for a psychotherapist/hypnotherapist, but she is hesitant to tell me her full story over the phone. I continue to talk with her, hoping to get a feeling for what she expects from hypnosis. Although I get all kinds of calls and requests, I never know how the conversation will go. I only know that if I can help, I will do so.

Sherry explains that she's feeling desperate. Her weight has ballooned to more than 180 pounds. "I don't know what to do," she cries.

I listen, then explain that my specialty is eating disorders. I offer her a consultation to determine the next step. I am rarely refused, for what I offer is hope.

Sherry arrives and when she sits down I notice she's nervous. Her body is visibly tight and guarded. She twists slightly away from me as she answers my questions. Her whole demeanor shouts low self-esteem and I detect an undertone of hostility, possibly due to her inner turmoil and struggle. Yet, I know she is vitally open to what I have to offer for she has shown an incredible amount of determination and courage by simply being here. From this I know our mutual adventure in the process of healing has begun.

We'll follow Sherry's quest to weight balance success throughout some of this book so that you can use her experience of the journey as a "road map" for what you might find along the way.

The Importance of Having a Star to Guide You

When I was growing up in the Puget Sound area, I had a life-changing experience as an eighth-grade student. In an assembly of eight hundred, I viewed a film that showed a street corner filled with businessmen dressed in dark gray suits. As they crossed the street in unison, the announcer's voice asked,

"Do you want to be just another gray-suited person conforming to the masses? Or do you seek a different kind of truth?".

This message is powerful. Even today it stands out as inspiration for everyone to go beyond what is known and commonly accepted. It inspires valuing and honoring what is unique and authentic for you as an individual. It implies finding a higher spiritual perspective to guide your life—one that is true to you.

On a personal level, it also confirmed my inner desire to make a difference in this world by following my heart and creatively blazing new trails. The realizations born from this experience became a pioneering vision—a star to guide me throughout my life.

The inspirational vision of a guiding star came from one of my closest mentors--my mother. When I was 13 years old, she gave me a framed poem entitled, "Ideals Are Like Stars" by Helen Steiner Rice.

The poem spoke to me about keeping morals, standards, and ideals high, as well as living a life based on truth. Steiner Rice's poem compared ideals to the stars in the sky, in that we can always reach for them and they will be there for guidance through dark times. By aligning my heart with high ideals, my life would also shine like a star. These thoughts and principles laid a firm foundation for me in my youth, inspiring and guiding me through some difficult teenage years.

Later when I divorced and went back to school for my master's degree, my mother sent the framed poem to me. I hung it in my office when I entered the business world for the first time at the age of 45. Every time I read that poem, it acted as an inner, guiding star to lead the way.

Each time I connected with its inner strength, I found I had vision and roots. Each time I set a goal, it was the absolute highest and purest I could set in light of the principles of this guiding star. Having a star to guide you is like having the Source of All Love bring you a fuller, more loving heart. Having an inner star for guidance led me to a purer awareness of love.

In this world, mentors, images, and the written or spoken word can be guiding stars to help everyone move through difficult life transitions. The simple act of reading this book can act as an inner star to guide you. Practicing the principles found within these pages can help navigate and smooth out the shoals of diet myths. You'll find anchor points of rest and reflection throughout these chapters as you voyage toward successful weight balance. In time you'll find hidden attitude keys which (when exercised) can unlock untold spiritual gifts hidden in the treasure chest of your life experiences.

This book can be an inner star to guide you when you regularly practice the techniques, exercises, and visualizations. In time, these components will help you tap into the pure love that already exists within you. This love burns with an eternal flame and can act as a guiding star or a lighthouse beacon, as you journey toward a more peaceful, contented life.

Take Inventory of Yourself and Societal Attitudes before Beginning the Journey

Many twists and turns convolute the path and the process when healing eating and weight issues. Each person's journey is unique, but certain behavioral similarities are fundamental at the start for nearly everyone who is affected. Why?

This may surprise you, but the sociocultural roots of diet and weight issues are hidden deep in plain view. They are found in the often unspoken and generally accepted expectations we hold about the world in which we live. These expectations are primarily determined by the combined attitudes of people who comprise this culture and society.

It is personally surprising to find out how deeply entrenched these sociocultural systems are to each of us.

Yet, taking stock of the conscious and unconscious influence these expectations hold on us individually is the first step to freeing ourselves from them forever.

To find out for yourself how immune or immersed you are in these biases, complete the *Checklist for Eating and Weight Issues* quiz by answering "yes" or "no" to the following questions. The results may surprise you, but they can also act as a catalyst and a wake-up call.

Checklist for Eating and Weight Issues

Have you ever:
(1) thought constantly about food or talked incessantly about dieting?
(2) felt overwhelming emotional stress?
(3) felt depressed with low self-esteem over several weeks, months, or longer?
(4) felt out of control?
(5) believed that all it takes to conquer weight issues is willpower?
(6) tried to restrict your diet to lose weight gained from overeating?
(7) felt guilty or ashamed about your eating habits or patterns?
(8) started eating, then found you couldn't stop?
(9) eaten so much at night that you could hardly get up in the morning?
(10) experienced relationship or family problems because of overeating, dieting, bingeing or purging?
(11) held high expectations or standards for yourself and others?

(12) told family what you *think* they want to hear about your eating habits, rather than the truth?

(13) maintained a lower or higher than average weight?

(14) gorged yourself, then used exercise, vomiting, or laxatives so you wouldn't gain weight?

(15) placed overt importance on your physical appearance?

(16) admitted physical appearance is of ultimate importance to your family and/or yourself?

(17) experienced swollen glands from vomiting?

(18) experienced menstrual irregularities?

(19) felt compelled to monitor what you or your children ate?

If you answered yes for one to five of these questions, then you've found this book at a good time. If you answered yes to five to ten questions, it's a wake-up call. Pay attention to the warning signs of weight issues now and begin seeking help. Implementing this book is a good first step.

If you answered yes to 10 to 15 questions, consider employing the help of a qualified therapist as you use this book, for the sake of your health and well-being.

If you or someone you know can answer yes to 15 or more questions, it's time for immediate action or a personal intervention. You can call the National Eating Disorders Association (NEDA) at (800) 931-2237 or contact *www.NationalEatingDisorders.org* for referrals and help. Your life or the life of someone you love may be at stake.

You will find hope, help, and the answers you seek by using this book and by contacting NEDA like millions have before you. In my heart, I know you will.

The Preliminary First Steps to Healing

The first step on the journey to healing is to take an inventory of where you are in relation to societal attitudes about food and weight. This you've already done by completing the *Checklist for Eating and Weight Issues* quiz. The next step is to make a commitment to become actively involved in the techniques, exercises, and process of actually living the principles outlined in this book.

---

*Once you make the commitment to "walk the walk,"
your life will never be the same again.*

As a good faith measure of your commitment, write down in your own words how you intend to implement the wisdom contained in this book through your actions every day.

I am willing to _____

_____.

Now that you've taken inventory and affirmed commitment to your goal, it's time to set the proper pace.

The Importance of Setting the Proper Pace

For me, finding solutions took many years of clinical experience and documentation. To my surprise, most of the wisdom and love came from the past seven years of practicing true inner balance.

If you're like I was in the beginning, you'll want all this wisdom as fast and as soon as possible. However, getting it fast can leave you with a case of spiritual indigestion—which will put you off the material indefinitely and ultimately defeat your progress. A ravenous style of questing can shock and overwhelm your body, mind, and emotions. A better and more balanced way to absorb this information is to allow yourself to learn by reading a chapter and then taking some time to merge its principles into your life.

Another way to proceed is to begin an ongoing series of book discussions that meet once a month with friends in your home or others interested in weight balance success in a private room at a local library. This pace allows you to devote a month of practice to the exercises and techniques in the book, sharing the harvest of wisdom you've gained from your collective learning experiences with the group. The exercises and techniques contained within these pages are surprisingly powerful when combined with this type of group support system.

Move gradually to each chapter, reviewing it nightly or weekly while continually doing the exercises that speak most pointedly to you or draw your attention. Most exercises or techniques can be done at least once. However, you can use them as many times as you want as you progress through subsequent chapters.

> *Give yourself a natural time boundary, or pace, in which to digest, review, and sustain your growth. This is the most loving action you can take for yourself.*

Routinely making new mini-goals or purpose statements for your weight balance success helps keep the adventure fresh and exciting.

You can return to any section in this book at any time and use it as a steady reference guide for change. The continual process of taking action, following through, and manifesting change empowers the divine you (Soul) to creatively transform any arena of your life.

The Next Step to Manifesting Your Goals

My golden invitation to you throughout this book is to explore with a light heart and a sense of freedom. Only you can make this grand adventure happen in the most enjoyable way possible. It all starts now when you turn the page with the expectation of being open to a new level of weight and balance success.

We'll begin by exposing and dispelling the social and personal culture surrounding eating and weight issues, exploring the validity or rhetorical hyperbole of these myths in depth throughout Chapter 1.

Part 1

Steps Toward Freedom

Chapter 1
Eight Diet Myths

The Diet Myth

Remember when you used to get the newest diet book in your hands, literally hot off the press? Guaranteed, it says. Guaranteed to work or your money back! "This time it's going to work," you think. "I just know it. It says so right here in print. Guaranteed!"

Although you've been here many times before, you still think this time is going to be the last. So many feelings are wrapped up in this moment. It's almost magical. A confluence of emotions race through you as you simultaneously experience the thrill of hope, success, approval, attention, and a feeling of rightness with the world. This time you know deep in your heart that you will do it right. "I'll be beautiful," you think. And then you're lost in a dream—a diet dream.

This is the basis of the insidious diet myth. We're led to believe that all our problems will be solved, all our dreams will come true—if only we diet. Even the word *diet* conjures up seemingly magical wishes and promises. Among these are hopes and dreams of future success about everything from beauty, self-esteem, feeling all right, being a good girl, as well as approval from others. But the diet myth is not magic. It is a lie.

Because it is silently sanctioned by society and tied in with equally misleading myths about being overweight, the diet myth continues to pervade society and is impervious to criticism. The combination of myths about dieting and the causes of overweight weave invisible threads that have the potential to knot up years of your life and wreak a megaton of damage to your health and well-being with time.

What's most frustrating is that one person can't change these societal beliefs (which are imbued as if they were the truth) for everyone. But one person *can* change their personal relationship to this propaganda for themselves—largely by seeing the diet myth for what it really is, gaining a truer understanding of its fallibility, and altering their response to it.

Seeing the Reality of the Diet Myth for What It Is

> *The reality is this: diets promising fast results create false hope.*

Women have been bound by this false hope for a hundred years or longer and now men are starting to buy into it. The truth is we have been and continue to be sold a misleading bill of goods that perpetually doesn't deliver on its empty promises.

For too long, myths about diet and overweight issues have been accepted as fact. Now you can free yourself and understand your feelings of hopelessness, confusion, and frustration—but *only* by first exposing the myths in their entirety. No more dieting to be beautiful, feel good enough, or feel better about yourself. No more dieting to gain the approval of family, society, or others. No more instant, dieting solutions to make everything better.

Take a deep breath now and bring yourself back to the present. It's time to take a gentle step across the realm of diet dreams. Take a gentle step toward real success with the secrets of weight balance contained in this book. Are you ready? The secrets are waiting for you.

The One Essential Quality to Develop for Weight Balance Success

> *One quality that you can develop, which will guide you*
> *through the misinformation of the dieting myths, is awareness.*

With awareness the secrets to successful weight balance will unfold as naturally and effortlessly as turning the pages of this book.

Finding my own awareness took years of digging. I first learned to dig for answers as a child of eight. One of my favorite things to do was to dig to the secret China Smuggling Caves from my Puget Sound backyard. I remember being outside, endlessly digging with a shovel in the backyard. My mother called me tenacious for I rarely gave up on what I wanted to accomplish or know. I wanted freedom even then and my spirit knew it.

Unfortunately only three years later I mistakenly applied my tenacity to my first diet. In 1957, I lost 16 pounds one summer at the age of eleven. I used my creative thinking to make up a diet. At that time, I'd encountered the concept of calories. I reasoned if I ate less, then I'd lose weight. Thus my first starvation diet was born. Believe it or not, I'd reward myself with an ice cream bar as needed. Does this sound familiar? That was my start on a dangerous cycle of dieting.

Later in life when I was in my late twenties, I disliked the ways I reacted to unhappiness by starving myself and calling it "my diet." In my thirties, I became worse. The more I tried to find answers in diets, the worse my unhappiness became. By the time I was in my forties, I was on the verge of self-destruction. What I learned from all this is it never works to diet—never!

What I found is that diet myths can be hypnotic in their persistent calling. I could not stop until I got to the bottom of the myths. It took me nearly thirty-three years to uncover the deceptions and discover the real answers I've found in weight balance.

Although my digging and searching certainly took me into the abyss of dieting, I wouldn't change one thing about my journey because each painful stumble and fall taught me more. Even though following each diet myth led me to another dead end, I would always discover a new direction or a new lesson to be learned. The uncovering process seemed like walking in a labyrinth for decades at the time, but with awareness I found freedom at the end.

The most important key I learned was this: *those who have found the way are best at showing others the way out.* Pathfinders who have been there before can map the invisible threads and untie the binding knots of diet myths. You too can chart your own personal journey.

In my practice I recently helped a formerly diet-bound woman let go of cravings, yo-yo dieting, and leave depression behind by using the processes explained in this book. We cleared myth after myth with these non-prescription techniques. All the while she was able to release the issues that kept her diet-bound. She is now off medication for depression and eating healthfully, with no cravings or compulsion to overeat. She's feeling good about herself and moving forward into a new career, loving herself and her life. *You can do it, too.*

Understanding the Roots of "Genetic" Societal Beliefs

Diet myths are a collective group of family experiences, which turn into beliefs and are then handed down for generations, in a metaphorically similar way that genetic traits are handed down. Through family connections, everyone has generally accepted myths. They are often built upon a consensus of group responses to life experiences and group wishes, rather than true wisdom. In accepting and embodying diet myths, false knowledge is distorted as truth and passed on for generations.

One example of this is reported in Ellen Ruppel Shell's book *The Hungry Gene*. The chapter called "Spammed" highlights the disastrous effects of group consensus on diet after World War Two.

Natives on a tiny South Pacific island of Korsrae were influenced by the perceived status of eating imported American fast foods. In time, their diets evolved from ones based on island-grown whole foods (fresh fish, breadfruit, mangoes and papayas which had kept their ancestors healthy for millenium) to ones based predominately upon canned Spam®, turkey tails, sodas, and beer.

Most of the children now have abscessed teeth and the adults expect to die in their fifties from diabetes, hypertension, and heart disease as a direct result of eating the imported foods. The nutritious breadfruit, mangoes and papayas that once ensured native good health now rot on the ground.

The Difference between Knowledge and Wisdom

The best education combines knowledge and experience, and bears fruit in hard-won personal wisdom.

We understand experience. But knowledge and wisdom are often confused in relation to diet myths. Knowledge can lead to wisdom when it is combined with awareness—when an individual is open to change with additional information and experience. Wisdom is the culmination of vast stores of knowledge based on experience (yours and others). It grows out of logical thinking, helping you understand how to make the best use of your knowledge and experience for the highest good of yourself and the world around you.

How do you take experience and knowledge to the level of personal wisdom? One way is by combining them with the practice of the techniques, exercises, and activities shared in this book. By digging at the logic and psychology upon which most of the diet myths are based, you'll discover true human needs are buried there. With awareness, you'll understand better the true source from which diet myths spring and the real reasons why they seem so irrefutable. Using that understanding with this book, you can expand your viewpoint to allow for the whole truth.

For example, you may discover when people hear you are on a diet, they are proud of you and you feel happy. You may realize the reason for this is the basic human need for love, acceptance, and approval.

Later when you're off the diet, you may find yourself defeated. The instant success is gone and you're still unhappy, only now you've added even more weight than before, due in large part to an unbalanced diet regime. Your needs haven't changed. Only now you know the truth about the diet myth—that it's all a lie. Now you're ready to take personal knowledge and experience to a higher level of weight balance wisdom.

You're now on the threshold of freedom from diet myths. The success you desire is just around the corner. Are you ready for the truth? Here are eight diet myths that bind the heart, which we'll explore in the rest of this chapter.

Myth 1: If I diet, my bad feelings will go away.

Myth 2: Dieting will make my world all right.

Myth 3: Dieting will make me beautiful.

Myth 4: Dieting will give me self-esteem and acceptance.

Myth 5: A diet makes me feel like a good girl.

Myth 6: Dieting will make others proud of me.

Myth 7: Dieting is just for a little while, then I can enjoy eating again.

Myth 8: Diets will work like magic to make life better.

Myth 1: If I Diet, My Bad Feelings Will Go Away.

In this myth, the idea is that going on a diet will make you feel good. The practical explanation is your attention is hooked into believing the myth and you expect to feel good *after* the process of dieting. How many times have you heard in conversations around you that being overweight isn't natural and a shame? The silent implication is "You need to lose weight."

You may then think, "If I lose weight, I'll be perfect. If I'm perfect, then I'll feel good. My feelings of shame, guilt, and frustration will go away as I lose weight. If only I could fit into a size 12, 10, 8, or even smaller. It will solve all my problems."

Once again, your attention is key. Placing your attention on a positive expectation works instantly to elevate your mood. However, what is *not* talked about is the reality of no attention put on how to get in touch with the healthy self-esteem required to get there. Without it, the emotional challenges of low self-esteem will always recur for you to deal with, even when you lose some weight. We'll explore some successful ways to use your attention for weight balance success in more depth in Chapter 6, under the subheadings *Practical Tools to Find More Answers* and *The Butterfly Technique.*

Myth 2: Dieting Will Make My World All Right.

It's easy to get caught in this myth. You may hear from family and the media that being fat is wrong. What is their definition of fat? Does their definition really apply to you? You may get caught into their judgment and then assume you are fat. This is also a situation of low self-esteem.

The next thought that accompanies this low self-esteem is, "If only I could lose weight, I'd be a better person and then my world would be all right." People at work will be more accepting of you, you reason. Mom, Dad, or husband will take the pressure off you. Yet life has a funny way of putting something else in our path to help us learn the truth. Discovering the truth will lead you to unshakable self-esteem.

> *Dieting myths based on misinformation that doesn't address personal well-being and self-esteem are quick fixes that only delay learning the real secrets to weight balance freedom.*

One patient told me she lost weight consistently for two years. She started a new life, fell in love, and married for the second time. After her wedding, she began gaining weight again. When I saw her, she wanted to lose the weight one more time. Her first purpose and primary reason for coming to see me was to lose the weight. Yet I soon discovered she was deeply depressed with serious thoughts of death.

When we talked further, she realized dieting never worked. Dieting in the past for her was up and down, and she always gaining back more weight than before *after she stopped dieting*. What was most shocking was her description of the diet she used to maintain a size 10 figure. She ate a salad a day. Sometimes she'd order a hamburger, which she'd then take home and eat only the meat patty. That's all she would eat—*daily*.

I asked her, "How do you expect to live if you starve yourself to reach a size 10 again?"

She told me, "Well, my husband bought me some expensive size 10 dresses. I have so many of them I want to be able to wear again." From her regime of starvation dieting, she weighed 135 pounds when they first met. It was the first (and only) time in her life that she was ever that thin.

She was on the road to discovering that proper weight balance meant giving her body the nutrients she needed. *Most importantly*, that meant eating three balanced meals a day. Other steps would follow on her road to healthy, active, balanced living. What she didn't yet understand is that her attention was still fixed on *starving to reach a size 10,* primarily in order to please others. Yet, living in more balance would eventually make her life all right and her weight would effortlessly reach just the right size. See Chapter 8 under the subheading *The Tinsmith's Escape* and *Moving Past Blockages and Denial* for more on this.

Myth 3: Dieting Will Make Me Beautiful.

How many of us have bought this myth? Remember how beautiful Marilyn Monroe was? She was a size 14. Now think of Twiggy in the 1960s. All of a sudden, television and fashion latched on to something new. A new image for women, only the new image seemed to say starving, deep-sunken eyes and a childlike figure are sexy.

This myth took only thirty-odd years to develop and take hold. It encouraged women to believe dieting to the size of a pubescent child is beautiful. Thus was born the myth dieting will make women beautiful (while displaying a child's figure as the ideal). But this myth leads to deprivation and inner dissatisfaction. I personally wonder who designs advertising based on this myth — pedophiles? I apologize for the shocking candor of this statement, but examining this question is the first step to discovering ways to disallow others outside of yourself from having this much control. We'll explore the power of asking the right questions in Chapter 3, under the subhead of *Learn How to Ask the Right Questions to Get Answers.*

At the pace of today's world, a myth can develop quickly. Each decade of communication builds upon group responses and group wishes ingrained by the previous one. In recent years designers have shown the heroin-chic look (a skin-and-bones image of near-starving models that appear drug-addicted).

This myth shows once again how corrupt images can have power over us, instead of empowering us to feel beautiful. Remember the saying, "Beauty is in the eye of the beholder?" An image of child addicts begins with subconscious general acceptance. This spells disaster with fatal consequences to generations of women and girls, for these distorted symbols of beauty subconsciously program or brainwash society into accepting the image or myth as truth. Decades later, fashion cycles back in again and the myth becomes even more deeply entrenched because it was so easily and unconsciously accepted the first time.

How do we, as women, want to respond? You can make a better choice right now. You can empower yourself by saying aloud, "I choose to break my old paradigms about dieting right now."

Myth 4: Dieting Will Give Me Self-esteem and Acceptance.

What a powerful illusion! This myth is like a dark, dirty window that hides endless, black, fearful, trapped feelings. A myth as dismal as this one leads to the false expectation that dieting can give you lasting self-esteem and self-acceptance. Yet, you end up failing each time—feeling you have no willpower, thus little self-esteem and low self-acceptance.

The truth is that this myth takes your real will away. It actually cuts you off from others while cutting you off from your own heart, separating you from your dreams of feeling good about yourself by perpetrating a lie—that the means to accomplish whatever you want is outside of yourself. It cuts you off from true self-acceptance, which is integral to real willpower. You end up paradoxically lonely and unhappy with yourself and your life.

> *Realize this right now: any mistake can be good when it helps lead you to learn more about truth and your true self. Truth is like a clean window that lets in light and allows you to see more clearly.*

The truth is this: *nothing* and *no one* can give you self-esteem and acceptance—only yourself. Real self-confidence and self-esteem always comes from within. It's a gift you give yourself with the help and grace of God. It comes in part from the experience of continually seeing yourself with all your strengths and courage clearly from the inside out. We'll explore this in depth in Chapter 9.

Myth 5: Diets Make Me a Good Girl.

This is what I call the "Parent Myth." Can you hear one of your parents in the background of your memories saying, "Be a good girl. That's right"?

Remember wanting attention from Mommy or Daddy? Your father may not have been around much of the time. When he was, he might have been tired from working all day. Do you remember him, off in the distance, too far away to talk to or reach? He may have been in his favorite chair watching television, but you weren't able to talk to him. He may have seemed just too distant. All you may remember is trying to be a "good girl." It's as if the voice of your parents is inside your head, saying "Be a good girl." All you wanted is to be noticed or acknowledged in some way.

If you combine this myth with the one that says dieting will make me beautiful, you might guess what your parents meant when they said be a good girl, which could lead to the birth of another myth—Dieting Will Make Me a Good Girl.

With the 20/20 vision of hindsight, you can see the many sides of the myth involved with Dieting Will Make Me a Good Girl. You may think that what you originally thought was the truth, yet the key is to look at the bigger picture and begin to see more.

To enhance your ability to see the bigger picture, I'll share the story of three blind men and the elephant. To find the essence of the elephant, each blind man felt a different part of it and described it to the others. The blind man at the tail described the elephant as a thin, long rope-like animal that hung in the air and moved side to side. The blind man at the elephant's ear described the elephant as a large flat creature that moved like a sail. The third blind man said the elephant was thick like a trunk of a tree since he only felt the elephant's leg. Which blind man was correct? Having a limited piece of truth or awareness can be misleading.

In connection to the myth of Dieting Will Make Me a Good Girl, those with sensitive natures and the very young will have a tendency to accept hand-me-down beliefs easily, taking on the beliefs of others as if they were the truth (though they are illusions).

> *As you read this book, the truth for your success will become clearer as you develop more compassion and understanding for yourself.*

You already have the ability to recognize illusion. You do so every time you watch a movie. You *know* it's just a movie. The aware part of you knows you're not only just watching a movie; you're also in a theater and you'll leave the theater after the movie is finished. The aware part of you recognizes the bigger, whole picture of life, not just a single part.

In a similar vein, your awareness has the ability to easily see through all the dieting myths listed here and any new ones you can imagine. You'll find out more and explore this amazing ability you already possess in Chapter 6 (*Tips for Getting Unstuck and Moving Beyond Discouragement*) and Chapter 10 (*Visit a Museum Technique*).

Myth 6: Dieting Will Make Others Proud of Me.

This story, from the American West, is about an eagle's egg that was placed in a hen's nest by a Blackfoot Indian brave. When the egg hatched, the eagle was raised as a chicken. It grew up believing it was a chicken. It pecked and scratched in the dirt, just like the other chickens. Fully grown one day, it saw a beautiful eagle soaring high in the sky. The eagle asked the old grandmother chicken about the beautiful bird that soared in the sky. The grandmother chicken said to stop wondering about things that weren't chicken business. So the eagle continued to scratch in the dirt and the grandmother chicken was proud of the way he listened to her.

Dieting often keeps you occupied with "the chicken business" of making others proud of you. This myth is a trap to keep you with your head down, busy pecking at the same useless diets which predominately define womanhood and keep you from fully realizing your full purpose and potential in life.

Now is the time to accept responsibility for being yourself and not react to other people's experiences, myths, emotions, or efforts to control you. This act is being the *cause* in your life (the source of true self-confidence), not the *effect* of others' attitudes and beliefs (a slave to myth). With full understanding of this knowledge, gained from reading Chapter 10, you can reach for freedom and be released from diet myths.

Myth 7: Dieting Is Just For a While, Then I Can Enjoy Food Again.

How did this myth become truth for so many women? I hope you question what we have heard as truth from advertisers for years from the point of view that diets never work. I had the misfortune to buy into dieting myths from age 11 to age 44—especially the myth telling me "dieting is just for a little while, then I can enjoy food again."

With this myth the focus is on food constantly. Too busy thinking about what we can and cannot eat, there's no time or energy left for building self-esteem or fully living life. By buying into this myth I found I never truly enjoyed food for thirty-three years.

The empty promise that I could eventually enjoy food again never happened for me. I experienced anxiety associated with the act of eating and preparing food, which only increased every year or two.

From my experiences, I came to realize truth comes on many levels. Others may have different views based on their family values and beliefs. For example, some families believe dieting promises that preach fast, easy weight loss or your money back. For those who believe it, their imaginations have created desire on a low level of reality. The key is to recognize how this type of thinking catches your attention but never works because the physical world in which we live runs on certain universal laws which are as immutable as the Laws of Physics. We'll explore these more fully in Chapter 8.

Secondly, this myth of Dieting Is Just For a Little While, Then I Can Enjoy Eating Again, can be viewed through attitudes. This myth puts you face to face with a choice between two statements. One says, think about dieting for a short time and the other says, then you can enjoy food again. The truth is dieting never works *when you go back to eating in the old ways.* Weight naturally comes back again with old eating habits, especially when it's combined with a lethargic metabolism which is often the legacy from most diets. An attitude adjustment about the kind of results you want—short-sighted or longer lasting, healthy ones—will help alleviate this situation. We'll explore this further in Chapters 3 and 4.

Myth 8: Diets Will Work Like Magic to Make My Life Better.

The greatest enemy of truth is the myth of how things seem to look versus reality. To illustrate, think about the following question: is a glass of water half-empty or half-full? Which is true? In some cases, both answers are true. The only difference is in the point of view or attitude, and *that* can make all the difference in the world, as shown in the following story.

Two women were having soup at a luncheon counter. One ordered a cup of soup and the other ordered a bowl of soup. One woman looked the cup and bowl and said, "I believe the cup and bowl have the same amount of soup in them."

"Nah!" said the other. So they asked the waitress to bring two empty glasses. They poured the soup from the cup into one glass and the soup from the bowl into the other glass. Both were exactly the same amount. The first woman said, "See, you're paying more for a bowl and you aren't really getting more soup."

The second woman got irritated and said, "I don't care. I want the bowl of soup."

We often determine the value of what is advertised by its appearance and presentation. If diets say you can lose weight in a hurry, then it's magically believable. The image is an illusion to get you to buy the false promise of the quick fix, which only looks good on paper. We'll cover and explore better ways to use your resources for weight balance success, which ties into attitude and viewpoint in Chapters 4 and 10 (*Understanding Your Personal Cycles Technique*).

All the diet myths you've read about are one illusion after another. Now is the time to reaffirm the commitment you made from the writing exercise in the introduction. Use it as an opportunity to carry you further into the next chapter as you discover five-plus passkeys for weight balance success.

Chapter 2
Five-Plus Passkeys to Ensure Success

Tips for Breaking through the Traps That Bind You

In an article from *Treatment Today* (reprinted in the October 1998 issue of *Reader's Digest*), Robert Epstein, a professor at the University of California, and his students surveyed more than 2000 years of self-change techniques.

I've distilled the results of his study and analysis into the following five principles. Adopting this approach is the easiest and fastest way to change your personal habits and start using this book for weight balance success.

> *When you take action and apply these steps to your life and personal situation, you join countless others who have reaped the benefits in effective results. Everyone who has tried them is heartened by the powerful way they work to manifest positive change.*

Passkey 1: Set Up Your Environment for Success.

I accomplished writing this book, even after working 60-hour weeks, simply by putting my word-processor within two feet of my bed. When I returned after 12-hour counseling days, it's the first thing I saw. My love for getting this book to you was all the additional motivation I needed to write daily. Changing your environment to facilitate positive change is a powerful catalyst for success.

People who change their eating habits by growing fresh herbs or vegetables in their dining room or kitchen windows illustrate one way to set up your environment for success. With fresh herbs growing so close, it's easy to reach for them to perk up meals with color and delicious, just-picked goodness and flavor—instead of reaching for canned goods, a high-calorie snack, or a frozen entrée that you can pop in the microwave oven.

The power of *changing your environment for the better* has proven results. Many psychologists first rediscovered and taught this technique in the 1960s with excellent results. I suggest you give yourself this gift by saying, "OK, I'll do that." Only *you* can do this for yourself.

In another example, one woman wanted to attain more balanced eating by learning ways to put more love into her meals, instead of stuffing the food down quickly without gentle thoughts. She started to change her environment by buying place mats in her favorite colors. Every time she looked at the place mats on the kitchen table, she was uplifted. She also purchased a set of whimsical yellow dishes that make her smile as she prepares food. By setting up this environment change, she harmonized her meal preparations and eating rituals with the power of loving attention.

Nothing is more powerful and simple to do: change your environment in loving, thoughtful ways and life will start to change in response to this. Where will you put this book so you'll remember to give loving, thoughtful attention to the success of your weight balance dream?

Passkey 2: Commit to New Behaviors by Writing a Positive Purpose Statement.

I know what you're thinking. You'd like to put this one off. You could put the book down and forget to read more right now. Or you could conveniently "forget" a written commitment was even mentioned. However, if you really want to harness the power of the subconscious and make it work for you, it's necessary to make your goal concrete in the physical world first by writing it down.

When you write down your purpose statement and accept this technique, it will help make your endeavors effortless. You'll enlist the help of your subconscious and your weight balance ventures will be easier. It's all in your attitude, for the attitude you choose to hold makes all the difference in your behavior, the results, and the ultimate outcome.

In my practice, I show patients how effortless change can be. First, I ask them what they specifically want to change. Second, I help them state it in positive words. Third, I help them write it down. For example, when people want to lose weight, their purpose statements need to reflect this in a simple way that's easy for the subconscious mind to understand.

I'm sure you've heard most people only use three percent of the total brain consciously. The subconscious comprises the other 97 percent of the brain. This part of your brain controls success through creativity, image, and the unspoken communication between the conscious and subconscious minds. By learning and utilizing the techniques outlined in this book, you'll harness the full power of that extra 97 percent to aid in effortlessly reaching your goal.

Many steps exist in reaching any goal. To be successful, each step or part of the process needs to be predetermined and then accomplished one stage at a time. Keeping your goals in mind while taking one step at a time eventually allows you to accomplish your dreams.

Likewise the process of weight balance needs to be examined and understood as many small steps on the journey to achieving your goal. Part of the process is learning to value the small steps along the way as you develop patience with yourself and others, while giving yourself permission to keep moving toward success.

Let's take a look at how to write a positive purpose statement. The following technique will lead you specifically through the steps of how to do it. (A positive purpose statement is the foundation for successful change. If you try to include diet myth misinformation into your positive purpose statement, it will undermine your well-being and the effectiveness of your purpose, delaying your ability to attain real weight balance results and success.)

Making A Positive Purpose Statement—Your Map to Your Destiny

This is the foundation of your success. It's relatively simple to manifest what you want in your life, but it's important to be clear, specific, and put it in writing. Again, a positive purpose statement is a golden key to unlock successful change for you by enlisting the help of your subconscious mind.

The following steps will take you past the conscious, judging part of the mind that prevents progress or change. Please take your time with this exercise. It works if you take your time. For clarity in this example, we'll use the positive purpose statement Sherry chose for herself.

1. *Write on an index card, "I want to be successful and learn the weight balance secrets. I am on my way to being successful and learning them."*
2. *Think of a symbol that you see often or every day, such as your watch or your keys.*
3. *Close your eyes and place your attention upward to the center of your forehead. This is where insight occurs in your mind.*
4. *Imagine someone or something you love. Imagine the love you feel is filling and overflowing your heart.*
5. *Now conceive of a favorite sound. Take your time and imagine listening to that sound.*
6. *Next conceive of a favorite healthy smell.*
7. *Finally conceive of a favorite healthy taste.*
8. *Now silently remember the exact words of your purpose statement and your symbol. Give yourself time to let it integrate by quieting your mind. The action of doing this is the secret key to getting the subconscious on your side.*

Passkey 3: Self-Monitor Your New Behavior.

Research over the past twenty years shows that self-monitoring is the final step that works to change behavior. Nothing is simpler to do. To self-monitor, find a time best suited to your schedule and use it to read and practice what you learn from this book. Maybe it will be only 30 minutes a day or an hour. Keep track of the time you spend reading and practicing the techniques in this book by documenting it on your calendar or making notes about it in your journal every day.

These three powerful techniques are the first steps to attaining non-prescription diet success. The techniques, visualizations, and exercises in the remainder of this book will help ensure your continued success.

How to Effortlessly Stay Powerful in Attention and Attitude for Continued Success

Like learning to ride a bike, the process of weight balance begins as a mechanical one. First you learn to pedal, and then you learn to steer, and then you learn overall balance—all at the same time. By practicing putting them all together as often as it takes, you eventually get all the pieces of the process happening easily, effortlessly, and simultaneously. Once this happens, you start having a great time and feeling free.

Once you've mastered riding a bike, you don't need to think about the pedals, balance, or steering. You just do it! It's the same with the weight balance secrets. First learn the steps, then practice them, and finally they just flow together effortlessly. You don't have to think twice about how to do them. You just do it!

Two More Keys to Weight Balance Freedom

The two final passkeys to weight balance success, however, are not as mechanical as pedaling, steering, or balancing a bike. These two keys cannot be learned by drilling yourself. That's because they are of a spiritual fabric. The two keys vital to your success are attention and attitude. If you forget to use one or the other, nothing you or I can do will make the principles in this book work for you. It's like leaving off the handlebars of the bike and still expecting it to navigate.

Lacking correct attitude and attention, you'll just be going through the motions of trying yet another diet book. Poor attitude or improper attention leads to boredom and discouragement, which can lead to disillusionment that convinces you to stop reading this material and quit doing the recommended techniques, visualizations, and exercises. When attention and attitude are mixed well with the correct practical steps, you will attain weight balance freedom. If you have trouble with *Not Your Mother's Diet*, it will usually be with one of these three keys: attitude, attention, or practice.

Commit to using and studying this book with real interest, practice the techniques and the results can be outstanding. This is just one way of working with the "as if" principle. Acting "as if" is simply (1) believe the change has already happened, (2) release it to your Higher Power, and then (3) take responsibility to do the actions, habits, and behaviors that make it real for you in this physical world.

> *A word about your Higher Power: It is simply what you want it to be. For some people, this is God or the Christ Consciousness. It can also be the highest part of you (divine Soul), nature, or even divine love. Base your interpretation of this on what's most comfortable for you.*

Be sure to turn the results of your situation over to your Higher Power (another attitude key). Then, put in the effort to read this book and practice its techniques. It may take many steps before others recognize changes in you, but each step brings you closer to your dream of success.

Mastering the Subconscious Using Visualization

The following visualization exercise for success is designed to help you move beyond the conscious mind using pleasant images and thoughts that appeal to your senses and the right brain. It works for two reasons. First, by connecting you to pleasant colors, shapes, sounds, and memories, it helps bring all your positive energy to the experience, setting you up for success.

Second, it's a master key. Think of your mind as metaphorically well-guarded between the conscious and subconscious. Security between the two requires confirmation of identity or authorization before access is allowed. The master key for entry just happens to be encoded in an exciting memory, colors, shapes, sounds, smells and tastes that I refer to in the visualization. Ensure the success of your master key by using an exciting memory as well as color, shapes, sounds, smells and tastes that are memorable and pleasant for you in the following exercise.

*A **Visualization** Exercise for Success*

1. *First close your eyes and look up to the center of your forehead. This is where insight occurs in your mind.*
2. *Now remember a happy time in your life when something really exciting or thrilling was happening. Tune in deeply to the memory and pause for a moment. What thrilling or exciting event is happening? Notice the details in the experience. See the shapes and colors around you. Hear the sounds. Notice the air has a particular scent to it. Describe it to yourself. Notice a taste in your mouth and describe it to yourself.*
3. *Next conceive of yourself doing this visualization exercise daily. Think of a time when you can relax to do this visualization undisturbed for five minutes each day. Finally, see yourself in a location in your home, doing this exercise and feeling excited about it.*

Give yourself this gift: Commit to take the time each day to do this visualization exercise.

A Simple Way to Release Excuses That Controlled You in the Past

First and foremost, remember that you are a spiritual being. Your inner, spiritual Self is the true Self that always is. Between every excuse, action, or feeling of doubt exists a silent space where you can be your true Self. Think of the relationship that your mind, body and emotions have to your true spiritual Self is like a car that needs an excellent driver to take care of and properly operate and maintain it.

Another way to look at your true spiritual Self is to view it as true attention. Other names for attention could be awareness or viewpoint. Being aware of where and how you focus your attention is finding your true, authentic Self. Think of this Self as beautiful, light, flowing, flexible, and yet extremely disciplined—like an ice skater or a dancer.

Go ahead and do the following exercise to get in touch with your true Self, either upon awaking or just before falling asleep. You can choose to either play the tape or simply run through the steps of this visualization exercise in your mind as you follow it.

First of all, your physical body will fall into a deep relaxation. Your thoughts and personality will quiet down to a restful state. By the count of ten, you'll reach a deeply relaxed state of consciousness. Following this, you'll have an experience as your true Self. When you are finished, you'll awaken feeling refreshed, alert, and good.

Touching Base with Your True Self

1. *Begin by saying, "I am going into a deep relaxation state to experience my true Self by counting from ten down to one."*

2. *Begin counting down now, saying each number upon your exhale. 10 . . . 9 . . . 8 . . . deeper and deeper . . . 7 . . . 6 . . . that's right, deeper into relaxation . . . 5 . . . even deeper . . . 4 . . . it's safe to have your experience . . . 3 . . . relax deeper . . . 2 . . . let everything go . . . and . . . 1 . . . That's right, you're completely relaxed.*

3. *Visualize yourself in a perfect garden, a place you may have visited before, seen in a picture, or just created right now. Perhaps it is an expansive area of lush green grasses with rose arbors, purple clouds of lilacs, flowering pink cherry blossoms, and ponds with banks of brilliant wild flowers. One area might host a thick, round lawn of chamomile flowers. Make your garden as simple or complex as you like.*

4. *Place yourself in the garden after you have completed visualizing it. See yourself take a walk, smell the flowers or gather a bouquet. At one point, you decide to rest on the inviting chamomile lawn. As you sit, notice the fruity aroma and breathe it in deeply. Chamomile, known for its ability to soothe the nervous system, lets you relax even more. Sink into the yielding perfume and softness of the lawn. Look down at your true Self and note what you see, sense, or hear.*

5. *Feel vibrantly refreshed and energetic. Do something fun: run, swim in a nearby pond, or dance among the flowers. Hear your favorite music. Bring others to your experience. Have an adventure.*

6. *When it is time to come back by the count of ten, you'll easily remember the feeling of your true Self experience. Feel free to return at a pace that's comfortable for you . . . 1 . . . 2 . . . 3 . . . 4 . . . 5 . . . 6 . . . 7 . . . 8 . . . 9 . . . 10. Welcome back!*

Write down what you experienced as your true Self. Next time you practice this visualization, you will experience even more of your true Self.

Now let's move your attention to three different reasons you have for continuing to read this book. For example, remember when you first thought about buying this book. Consider when you'd like to read this book tomorrow. Next, imagine yourself balanced and at a healthy weight, feeling good about yourself. Can you do that? The part of you that remembered, thought, and imagined, is *your true spiritual Self.* Write down three reasons for continuing to read this book.

(1) _____

(2) _____

(3) _____

Getting Ready for True Success

True success is right around the corner. It's your privilege to discover it for yourself. How do you do this? First, by looking with a true heart at the automatic excuses you normally use to avoid following through on your intentions. What are your most frequent excuses? If you can write them down this will lead you to the next step. Take a moment to write them down.

(1) _____.

(2) _____

(3) _____

Ask yourself, do I really want to be stubborn, tied fearfully to my excuses? Or do I want to experience freedom and success? book text, book text book text.

> *By distracting your attention from these excuses and asking questions about a possible scenario of freedom and success, you set up curiosity about an alternate future.*

Like a story that's only half-told, once your curiosity is engaged, you've just got to see how the story ends. It's on this principle that you, as your true spiritual Self, can start and proceed toward success.

Using your curiosity right now means being willing to put the book down for five to ten minutes to do the next exercise. This exercise will teach you how to get ready for true success. Find a quiet place where you can lean back right now for ten undisturbed minutes.

> *A Loving Technique*
>
> 1. *Close your eyes and place your inner attention on an imaginary spot between your eyes. This is where insight occurs in your brain.*
> 2. *Next silently ask to connect to your Higher Power, as you know it. Some people believe their Higher Power is God; others experience their Higher Power as the highest part of themselves. Choose whatever truth is best for you and connect with it while doing the exercises, techniques, and visualizations in this book.*

3. *Next, pick a word that means or feels like love to you. It could be the name of a loved one or a beloved pet. If it's the right word, you will feel love. This is the most important indicator and part of this technique.*

4. *Say or sing the word to yourself for five minutes. Most people who do this are at first surprised to find out how long five minutes takes. You might set a timer or your watch if needed.*

5. *Your mind may be actively running thoughts in your head, like monkeys doing tricks. Just let those monkey-like thoughts run by as if it was a television program. You'll soon become bored with them and your mind will calm down shortly.*

6. *Notice your breathing as you sing your love-word, and notice how your body begins to calm down.*

7. *Next ask yourself, what is a balanced, healthy weight for me? Trust yourself to know exactly what is best for you as a healthy weight. Use the space given at the end of this chapter to write that down now. The sentence starts with "I am on my way to _____." For one person the statement might be "I am on my way to being (fill-in-the-blank) pounds." For another, the statement might be "I am on my way to being a size (fill-in-the-blank)." What's important is that it's your purpose statement, you write it down, and you accomplish it in small steps.*

8. *Go to the last page in the chapter now and write down what you received. Be bold enough to push through any hesitancy or lethargy you may feel about doing this right now. Just do it to ensure your continued success.*

9. *Close your eyes again and sing or say your love-word three more times. Fill yourself with love and contemplate the weight you wrote down. Explore how comfortable you are with it as you imagine how you will feel at that weight.*

10. *Next, imagine a symbol that represents your purpose. One symbol that works for some people is a rainbow. Another symbol is a sunrise or a rose. Trust yourself to know exactly what is right for you to choose as the symbol of your success. Make it personal and meaningful for you. Pick one symbol and when you sing your love-word, imagine your symbol too. Again, use the space at the end of this chapter to write down the symbol of your success. When you are finished, close your eyes and sing your love-word three times. Say to yourself, "It is blessed in love; it is filled with love; it is finished in love." Take three deep breaths and open your eyes.*

Sherry, a compulsive dieter, chose a white dove to represent herself on the way to eating healthfully in just the right amounts to fit into a size 16. She is on her way to seeing herself at this goal, *walking more and loving it* with joyful feelings—the way she feels when she laughs. This is a beginning step for her on the way to her destination of weight balance.

If you skimmed through this part of the book without using the tape or doing the exercise, I urge you to stop and carry through with it right now.

> *Know that there is no right or wrong way to do it. Like making bread, you can stir it any way you choose, just as long as you stir it and get the job done.*

Just do it now. Go to *Guidebook Questions to Contemplate and Journal* in this chapter. As you go through each item, write down what you receive.

The importance of doing this exercise and carrying through by writing it down cannot be

emphasized enough. Think of it this way: What if you were baking some wholesome bread for

your family and later discovered you forgot to put in the leavening agent? Would the bread rise?

It probably wouldn't turn out as well because you forgot one of the most important ingredients.

> *The techniques, exercises, and activities in this book are clearly the metaphorical leavening agent that brings healthy weight balance success.*

Guidebook Questions to Contemplate and Journal

1. What do I want? I want _____
2. Now rewrite what you want and make it failure-proof. For example, if you wrote, I am on my way to losing ten pounds, rewrite it as "I am on my way to being *lighter and lighter as a size* (whatever size is healthy for you while discounting the weight myths)." It is important to write it as a formula or an exact recipe, using these words: "I am on my way to being _____." Then fill in the blank according to what you want.
3. Now write the purpose statement again. Start your sentence by writing the exact wording, "I am on my way to being _____" and finish

the sentence with your exact written purpose statement from the first question. Write it in the blank lines provided.

_____

_____

_____

4. My personal symbol of success is _____

_____

_____

To review:

1. Commit to singing your love song to yourself each day at the same time daily.
2. Imagine yourself seated comfortably and relaxed, doing that now. See yourself in the room where you'll be.
3. Change something in your environment to help you remember to do this for yourself. Tell yourself, "I deserve to do this for me."
4. Think of a beautiful sound. Then imagine a wonderful smell and think of a favorite taste and color.
5. Now close your eyes and sing your love-word to yourself as you imagine your loved one, the beautiful sound, the wonderful smell, a favorite taste, and let go as you accept love flowing to you. Briefly record your experience in your journal.
6. Did you use feelings to describe your experience? Did you use thoughts to describe your experience? Did you describe how your body felt doing this? Rewrite it again using feelings, thoughts, and body sensations.
7. Remember to (a) set up your environment for success, (b) commit to new behaviors by writing a positive purpose statement, (c) self-monitor your new behavior, and (d and e) focus your attitude and attention on your commitment.

When Beginning Something New

When you first try something new, it's natural to have mixed feelings about it. Often inner conflicts are revealed. For example, sometimes when people try these techniques for the first time, they write, "I felt I was doing it wrong. My body couldn't relax." It's okay if this was your experience. It's fine for a first step. As a springboard into the next chapter, try the following journal activity.

Think of an area of your life occupied with inner conflicts. This can be any situation you've had mixed feelings about. Next, write down your feelings about the situation. For example, confusion and anxiety are two emotions that can revolve around inner conflicts.

Now draw a picture of those feelings. You can pretend you don't know how to draw when doing this exercise. Draw a funny stick drawing or doodle your feelings. This will help you release them by engaging the subconscious mind.

Lastly, make a positive change in the picture. It's all right for the drawing to turn out any way it does. If it makes you feel better, then you've helped give a voice to some of the inner conflicting feelings you have about the situation. This activity helps clear away some feelings (by using the unlimited perception of image and the nonjudgmental aspects of the right brain to get them down on paper,) so the logical verbal language centers of the left brain can eventually express what you feel through journal writing.

Where do these conflicted feelings come from? What's the true meaning behind them? More importantly, what can we do about them? We'll explore these questions and more as we discover ways to break through the emotional traps that bind us in Chapter 3.

Chapter 3
The Dieting Trap

The Diet Paradigm on a Social Level: More Than Fifty Years in the Making

Sherry wondered aloud about how the diet paradigm had gotten the firm hold it has on society today. Let's examine recent history by scanning aspects of the last fifty years.

During World War II, the threat of European-based dictatorships splashed across the headlines of nations. The people of the world perceived the dictators in power as domineering and manipulative of others. Many feared for their lives and faced the real possibility of the total annihilation of their people. In the United States, mothers supported the war effort by working in factories.

When the war ended, a great publicity effort turned women back to their homes so jobs would be freed up and available for the men returning from overseas. The homemaker role was glorified and best epitomized in the new television shows of the day, such as "Father Knows Best" or "Leave It To Beaver."

The widespread influence of television shows like these began to indoctrinate girls from the baby-boom generation from a very early age by encouraging them to strive for the 1950s ideal: picture-perfect life situations and personal appearances that mirrored what they saw on these television programs.

The reality behind the scenes was that families struggled to live up to the two-dimensional, superficial images of the happy households they saw on television. This resulted in denial and stuffing real emotions to keep up the appearance of the television families, breeding personal confusion and resentment among family members for being unable to attain this perfect image and unable to express their true feelings about it.

The long-term result of denial and swallowing real feelings within the family unit is that the situation continued to worsen in subsequent decades. Family members erupted in negative, self-defeating behaviors, such as overeating, out-of-control shopping, alcohol and drug abuse, and escapism into even more hours of television viewing. All this simply supported more living-in-denial to avoid addressing real-life problems and issues. Who would guess that generations of loss during the Great Depression and two World Wars would predispose the people of this nation to become willing participants to television's hypnotic influence and the sedative world of entertainment it offered?

Not only did television distract and entertain us, it even told us which products to buy, eat, use, and wear. The idea of molding every woman to a feminine ideal helped divert everyone's attention and placed more importance on consumerism to uphold outer appearances. Who could have predicted that the influence and manipulation of trends through image would spread so far, so fast, and so thoroughly and that our future would be altered forever by television?

Baby Boomers in the Cross Hairs

The years 1951 to 1957 focused on rebuilding the economy and the world after the war. In November 1957, a monthly general interest magazine named *Cosmopolitan* focused on the question "Are Teenagers Taking Over?" For the first time in history, teenagers had money to spend. Since their parents had lived through years of lack during the Great Depression, they wanted to give their children more of the good life, the things they never had.

The New Yorker picked up the trend that month and printed, "These days, merchants eye teenagers the way stockmen eye cattle." During this time teen magazines became an important influence and element of teen subculture.

By 1960, more than a dozen magazines had slanted their marketing toward teenage girls. By the end of 1963, the British Invasion and the musical revolution began making a mark internationally. Teenagers expressed their natural rebellion through new fashion standards when Mary Quant defied the status quo with the Mod look and the mini-skirt. *Seventeen* magazine then featured them. Soon more teen magazines began to feature these fashion trends.

As a natural part of the rebellion experience and wanting their own identity, teenagers looked for a new image. Initially Twiggy was discovered for her face but was considered too skinny to model. However, her popularity increased by 1966. I remember the influence Twiggy had on me when I modeled for the January issue of *Seventeen* that year. I lost weight until I was below 100 pounds in order to feel thin enough. Other girls and women copied Twiggy in the decades that followed.

The 1962 release of Rachel Carson's *Silent Spring* inspired the ecological, back-to-nature, co-operative movement, which grew in the 1970s when certain segments of the US population began to express renewed interest in health, nutrition, and organic foods. A portion of the general public recognized the relationship between mind, body, Spirit, and the quality of the food we ate.

But the Twiggy image of thinness still equaled "health" in the mind of mainstream fashion magazines. The voluptuous image of Marilyn Monroe as the feminine ideal was gone and so was acceptance of flesh in commercial images.

Overtly critical judgment of others tracked the trend of thinness. Already beautiful models' good looks were further enhanced with photographic touch-ups. Plastic surgeons plied their craft of body sculpting in their quest to perfect their conception of what the feminine physique should be. Eventually, mass consciousness working through mass media led to more emphasis on controlling the feminine with outward perfectionism being the driving behavioral force and primary goal.

Yet despite this, the consciousness movement grew, bringing with it the energy of cooperation and compromise. Those who were interested in spiritual matters began deep explorations within to find the most basic values of their innermost selves. Awareness about how the modern world had systematically polluted the air, water, and land grew. In the arena of diet, investigation into what advertising influences had done to corrupt the mind/body image and glimpses of how they had directed the feminine body ideal became conspicuous.

Exposing the Illusion

The struggle to be free of the mass-marketed illusion is a process similar to what the butterfly goes through when freeing itself from a chrysalis. What I strive to do in this section is shine light on how the diet paradigm evolved—with the intent of helping readers break free of the illusions it casts.

To further expose the illusion for yourself, take time to leaf through a fashion magazine and view present-day advertising images while keeping the previously mentioned history in mind. Notice what kinds of bodies top fashion designers employ to display their creations. Ask yourself: Which movie stars have had ribs surgically removed in order to permanently alter their waist measurements? Who is surgically altering other body parts or areas in order to appear slimmer, tighter, or forever young? Digital computers and retouched photographs improve images, magically giving models fuller breasts. Undoubtedly, healthy-looking, athletic images of women abound, but they fall mainly on the low-flesh side.

Where is acceptance of variety and individual beauty?

What do natural, healthy women need to do in order to value themselves for what's inside?

The answers to these questions can lead to a deeper awareness of who you really are and where you stand on the topic of buying into the Hollywood or Madison Avenue images for women.

How the Dieting Cycle Begins on a Personal Level

A little girl, about seven or eight years old, wants to get parental attention in the worst way. She wants to be noticed, soothed, or protected from the emotions of her childhood psyche. She wants to be closer to her parents, but how?

Maybe she sees her mother enjoying something, eating a meal or preparing breakfast on the weekends. Her father might be relaxing with a beer or cocktail. Maybe he takes his little girl for an ice cream during a special time when she gets to go with Daddy. Maybe the special times she remembers sharing with her mother were surrounded by food experiences.

It's possible that as the little girl grows up, classmates tease her for being fat. Or maybe she just has self-conscious feelings about plumpness because Daddy talks disparagingly about obese women or criticizes her mother for putting on weight. Maybe the remarks from her father or the teasing of her classmates provoke an angry response in the little girl. What does she do?

Since little girls are taught it isn't nice to express or feel anger, this little girl learns to swallow it. Yet the hostility flashes deep inside her for a moment before it's swallowed. The hurt and betrayal she feels may also be swallowed so fast that they're nearly forgotten. And almost without a thought, the swallowed anger seems to magically go away.

Yet the result of swallowing anger (or any other strong emotion for that matter) is that eventually it comes out sideways in unconscious, uncontrolled behavior. The primal feelings of anger and betrayal that are swallowed become scattered through the subconscious, resulting in confusion. What happens to the little girl?

She grows up and—like Sherry—thinks it's paramount for her to focus on the feminine diversion of diet worries or the hunt for the perfect body. This is how the personal dieting cycle is born.

The Wisdom of Honoring Your Emotions

Emotions are often misunderstood. They are seen as negative outbursts that are best repressed. But strong emotions can be a way for your intuitive self to get your attention when you're in the midst of a situation.

> *Your intuitive self uses emotions to flag a situation and bring it to your attention, so that you can take a deeper look at the truth.*

A heightened sense of awareness can help you discern what's happening on a deeper level, so you can make the best-informed decision about what's right for you in that situation.

Once you listen to the deeper truth underneath your emotions, you'll know what the truth of a situation is. Then you'll be calm and relaxed, responding from your true Self when choosing your course of action. Emotions can be important intuitive indicators that help you evaluate situations—*but only when you stay in touch with and honor your true Self from moment to moment.* The important thing is not to hold on to, or stay stuck in, any emotional state but simply pass through it to the higher ground of a greater understanding of what is true for you.

This can only happen when we first acknowledge the emotions within ourselves and see them for what they truly are—indicators—instead of denying, ignoring, squashing down, or swallowing how we really feel.

What to Expect When You Take New Actions

It's normal to feel conflicted and uneasy when you start to take new actions in your life and break old habits or thought patterns. Many people know the best course of action to take to improve their lives (such as reading and applying the principles in this book). But knowing and doing are two different things. When they do take action, it often causes the reverse of what they expect to happen. Instead of everything getting better, they may feel empty, hurt, angry, or aggressive inside.

The truth of it is this: first it gets worse and then it gets better. If you don't fight or repress your feelings, but rather accept them as a natural part of the process, you'll be on your way to dealing with your emotions in a healthier way sooner.

It's relatively easy for someone who doesn't know this to go back and get stuck in the same old habits and patterns when they're in doubt. Yet it's all a matter of breaking through the illusion of childhood loss and fear.

When you let go of a past habit or way of being, you may experience the change as loss. But by knowing what to expect emotionally at the outset, you can calmly reassure yourself that there is nothing to fear. Unlike others who get caught up in doubt, you know your purpose and goals. You can stay centered and clear while focusing on learning more skills and tools from the techniques offered in this book.

Remember first and foremost, you are a tremendous spiritual being. You can decide to take new, positive actions with the expectation that you'll feel sad or empty at times, knowing this will pass as part of the process of letting go. It doesn't matter if the change is large or small; the process of letting go is the same for both.

For example, when we experience the death of a loved one, religious rituals help us accept, let go, and cope with it. We attend funerals to help us surrender to the reality and assist us in fully accepting what has happened. Friends and family show support and sympathy for us. Crying at funerals helps release some of the grief by giving it a voice.

Our physical bodies and emotions need to be honored similarly in any letting go process. This honoring process helps empty and clear out old behavior patterns and ruts in our thinking. Support from friends also helps with this process. Just remember that emptying out the old makes room for the new, allowing more space for success to develop and grow.

Feelings Are a Golden Key

Not being fully connected to your feelings or misperceiving thoughts as feelings can create more confusion and miscommunication within you. The following activity shows one way to get better acquainted with your emotions. The goal is to become friends with your feelings, instead of treating them like the enemy. Even if you think you already know what you feel, try this exercise. You might be surprised to discover something new about yourself.

Look over the following *Emotions Awareness Chart* with the idea of befriending your emotions. When making new friends, we often make plans to spend time together. So spend some time doing the following: At the end of each day, at the same time every day, check off all the emotions you felt during the course of that day. After a while, you'll become more adept at recognizing and differentiating them. This is a first step to more fully recognizing your feelings, which can lead to building greater awareness. When subtler feelings emerge, add them to the list.

Emotions Awareness Chart

	Monday	Tuesday	Wednesday	Thursday	Friday	Saturday	Sunday
Annoyed							
Angry							
Aware							
Hurt							
Interested							
Used							
Withholding							
Repressed							
Willing							
Lust							
Content							
Threatened							
Scared							
Brave							
Safe							

Sad
Self-Punishing
Sincere
Numb
In Balance
Unloved
Loving
Helpless
Hopeless
Complete

At the end of the week ask yourself, what did I learn from my emotions? What greater truth were they trying to bring to my awareness?

For example, sometimes you can plumb the depths of your emotions (like anger) and find beneath it a real human need. One such need is the need to have more love in your life. Moving through anger and other emotions to acknowledge the deeper needs underneath brings you to the source of your truth and the cause level of your misgivings. Acknowledging and addressing the deeper truth and cause of your emotions (a need for love) has the potential to permanently alleviate anger at the source.

Be sure to write down the answer to the question "What did I learn from my emotions?" in your journal as a simple way to record your changing awareness and document your quest for the truth in writing. In a month, re-read your entries to review your progress.

If you'd like, draw a picture in your journal that represents the emotions you experienced that day at the end of each day. Lastly, be sure to make a positive change in the picture just before you finish it.

Three Myths Society Holds about the Cause of Obesity

In Chapter 1, we explored the eight myths individuals hold about dieting. Society also holds three stereotypical myths about the causes of overweight, which are then projected upon anyone who is considered fat or the least bit heavy for their height. They are, as follows:

Myth 1: Just eat less and lose weight.
Myth 2: Just exercise more and lose weight.
Myth 3: Just use more willpower (to eat less and exercise more) and lose weight.
Once we explore these in detail, you'll see why they're myths.

Myth 1: Just Eat Less and Lose Weight.

This myth assumes that people who are overweight or obese eat large amounts of food. Sometimes this is true, but not always. More often than not, many people who are perceived as fat eat less than their thin counterparts and still can't seem to lose weight, no matter how little they eat. What's really happening here? Why doesn't eating less work?

The answer is not necessarily in how much you eat, but in the quality of what you eat and in what proportions. Too many times people who struggle with weight issues miss essential macronutrients (proteins, carbohydrates, and fats) or micronutrients (vitamins, minerals, trace elements and enzymes).

The key is *not* necessarily in counting (and restricting) calories in foods you eat, but rather in *maximizing nutrition* in the foods you eat. Many people today are literally starving from lack of proper nutrition due to diets based on modern-day, highly processed foods. Most of these foods are so low in essential nutrients that they put people who base their diets on them within flirting distance of deficiency diseases.

Cutting back further on nutritionally inadequate and deficient foods only serves to slow and eventually shut down the body's natural ability to metabolize foods and effectively burn calories. In effect, the body switches to starvation mode.

Instead of burning stored fats, it begins to cannibalize itself by breaking down precious muscle tissue (protein) for the nutrients and amino acids that are crucial for life. Since retained muscle mass naturally and metabolically burns more calories than fat (even in resting states), losing any muscle mass further impairs the body's ability to metabolize nutrients and burn calories.

In the cannibalizing process, the body will pull vitamins, minerals, and other elements from the bones, muscles and other tissues if it's not getting them from food sources in the diet, leaving dieters prone to osteoporosis and other degenerative conditions and diseases.

> *For those who do tend to overeat, their behavior can also be viewed as nutrient starvation, as well as the mind game a chemical imbalance from lack of proper diet can play on people. The feeling of being out of control and acting out on it through uncontrolled eating are signs of lack of nutrition and nutritional starvation just as much as they are characteristic of deeper emotional issues with regard to food.*

The answer is not in restricting foods or eating less. Restricting only leads to panic and binge eating, which is a natural response to starvation or lack of any essential nutrients.

As an example, I'd like to share the story of Ann. "Look at me," she said. "I can stay on a diet and I've quickly lost thirty pounds in just a few months."

Yet Ann didn't realize that once she reached her goal, she'd throw out restrictive dieting and slowly start eating the way she used to eat. When you restrict your food, your natural instincts tend to want to binge or balloon out of control, to save the body from what it perceives as famine. This ballooning effect can be gradual as in Ann's story: a little ice cream treat one day, a double cheeseburger for lunch, and a rich dessert that night. Soon all the weight she lost comes back gradually and then some. What is the philosophy behind the balloon effect?

When you pinch the middle of a tube balloon, it simply balloons out in other directions. So restricting food only results in closet eating, binge-eating, or spending more than the overeater can afford for food after strict deprivation diets. The cycle begins to spin out of control because no amount of willpower to restrict or eat less food will work to sustain life over the long haul.

This may run its course in weeks, months, or years, until the next time you gather together the impetus to restrict your diet again. The "less food" concept leads not to permanent weight loss, but to yo-yo dieting, repressed anger, and a state of perpetual weight gain because of a chronically lowered and sluggish metabolism that tries to survive on nutritionally deficient foods.

How can you combat this? Choose to let go of the myth that eating less is the answer to your weight problems. In the beginning of Chapter 4, I'll share a resource that will help you customize your diet to your own nutritional needs, help stop cravings, as well as ensure optimum health, high energy, peak athletic performance—basically a way to stay young at any age.

Myth 2: Just Exercise More and Lose Weight.

The flip side of the eat-less myth is the exercise-more myth. The truth is that if you're not getting enough nutrition, exercise can be deleterious to your health. A metabolism sluggish from improper diet will not easily jump-start just because it's coerced with exercise. Many times the body will pull magnesium from the muscles and calcium from the bones when driven by exercise, causing even more of an imbalance and ultimately leading to more serious conditions, such as osteoporosis.

If you've been sedentary for some time, you may want to ease back into activity. It's important to do just the right amount of the right form of exercise initially to enhance your health and condition. Your overall weight can unconsciously pull you, like gravity, into the same old patterns of inactivity so it can take an effort to get started. Here's a gentle way to start manifesting a safe, gradual change into more activity.

Try this one half-hour before a meal: Choose to eat a healthy appetizer (a healthy complex carbohydrate, such as a glass of fruit or vegetable juice, some raw vegetables or fresh fruit; or a healthy protein, such as a few ounces of cheese or yogurt with a handful of raw nuts or seeds).

Then take a short walk around your home or office (six to eight blocks for a fifteen-minute stroll). Do this gently to begin erasing past habits of inaction. Start with one fifteen-minute walk per day and gradually increase it to two. Strive to reach the goal of walking for fifteen minutes before every meal. As you gain fitness over time, gradually increase your pace to a brisk walk and increase the number of blocks that you walk to ten to twelve each time.

This simple activity has the effect of jump-starting your metabolism over time. Since your ability to burn calories is already enabled by the brief exercise, when you return and sit down to eat you'll automatically process the meal much better and burn calories in your fat storage more efficiently.

If you combine exercise with a meal plan that focuses on foods geared to your metabolic type, you'll see even faster results in your quest for weight balance. (See Chapter 4 where we'll explore more on metabolic typing, and you can check out *The Metabolic Typing Diet* by William L. Wolcott with Trish Fahey.)

If you like the results you're seeing and feeling with mild walks before meals, in a month or two you'll easily be able to add a mild workout or two during the week. On one day of the week, try some easy cardiovascular movement, such as moving to music for 20 to 30 minutes.

Engaging in light weight-training two days later can help strengthen your bones, further reducing the potential threat of osteoporosis. An inexpensive way to weight-train and build your upper body strength uses water-filled plastic bottles for inexpensive weights. To avoid potential injuries, increase the amount of water in the bottles gradually over time as your strength increases.

I would be remiss if I didn't address those people who fall at the *other* end of the spectrum however—those who exercise to the extreme as a way to burn calories and keep weight off, as shown in the following story about Diane.

Diane is a typical dieter although her eating and exercise routines are fanatical. She would exercise morning, noon, and night in order to facilitate binge eating. Although her whole life is built around accommodating her eating and exercise habits, she doesn't see how much it affects her emotional state, relationships with family and friends, job performance, or what she does in her spare time (when there's spare time left after excessive exercising and overeating).

Diane bought the myth of exercising more to lose weight because of a fantasy. Primarily, she wanted to look like her favorite ultra-thin model. At first glance, the myth of exercising more to lose weight seemed to satisfy her in that this is what she believed she needed to do to attain her desired results. Soon Diane was on her way to becoming her model-thin fantasy.

Diane's thoughts and attitudes were not grounded in the real world when she was binge exercising however. Her daydreams progressed to fantasizing about getting revenge, winning, and being on top of the world. For a little while, Diane pretended that her dreams and fantasies would come true, until the pain of overeating and excessive exercising brought her back to the present. The reality is that Diane had to cancel a date she was looking forward to once again, because she binged and then exercised herself into exhaustion. She wound up being too sick and too tired to go on her date. This happens more often than Diane allows herself to acknowledge.

Yes, regular exercise is healthy for everyone. It's when the will or ego starts manipulating how much you exercise, how long you exercise, or how often you exercise that problems can surface. Thirty minutes of specific body exercises or aerobics a few times a week are good for your health and cardiovascular system.

A healthy self-esteem goal for your exercise routine is good health and a stronger body (not necessarily to lose weight). You can choose to be healthy, strong, and maintain a balanced weight with exercise and eating right.

An additional 30 minutes of walking at the end of the day is relaxing and one of the best ways to keep your body moving and healthy. Think about inviting a friend or spouse for a relaxing walk along the beach, down city streets, or around the local park in your neighborhood. Who would you love to share this with? Who might you meet and what might you see? What natural adventures can you have during this time?

Now shift your perspective and think about *having* to take a walk, from the viewpoint of thinking you have to exercise more. Think of forcing yourself to walk from fear of not losing weight or fear that someone will once again comment about your weight.

Worse yet, you might be angry about those comments and you don't even recognize it. You might be so used to denying anger that you don't know when it's healthy to express it. It's natural to be angry with anyone who makes snide comments about your appearance. You might be seething deep inside, yet you don't even recognize that you are angry because you automatically channel your anger and energy into exercise. Allowing old attitudes and stubborn behaviors to take charge and entice you to binge with exercise is hostility turned upon yourself—self-punishment by exercising to the extreme. Choose instead to think of exercise as inviting and relaxing.

Make a choice and choose to let go of past behaviors and attitudes today. Embrace choosing to trust in positive outcomes and choosing to trust yourself. We'll explore this concept of trusting yourself and positive outcomes more through an exercise in Chapter 6.

Myth 3: Use More Willpower (to Eat Less and Exercise More) and Lose Weight.

The third myth combines the first two myths and just adds willpower. If the first two myths didn't work alone or together, they won't work when combined with more willpower.

This myth emerges when people feel hopelessness, helpless, useless, and don't know consciously what to do with their power. Many of them automatically act in ways to exert control over their bodies.

When you're feeling out of control and panicked, more willpower isn't going to push back tides of past controlling behavior. More willpower can't hold back the tides of emotions, especially the anger and hurt that led to overeating and comfort foods. Willpower can't hold back the illogic of societal beliefs and myths.

The myth that you need more willpower over your food or your behavior is completely misdirected. This is comparable to the way that you can only hold your breath for so long before you have to take the next breath.

The instinctual urge to breathe is the same as the urge to eat. Both are vital for life. The instinctual subconscious can drive you to eat when your anger is so repressed that you're about to self-destruct. More willpower, or control in any way, only heightens repression and the urge to eat. More willpower just doesn't work.

What *does* work is building up your self-esteem so that you feel more adequate and more encouraging of yourself, so that you have the inner power to make different behavioral choices that set you free. You *can* choose to release old, controlling, willful ways and make new choices. We'll explore the fact that you have a choice in how you respond in more depth in Chapter 6.

Later in this chapter, I'll give techniques for recognizing and addressing feelings before they get the better of you behaviorally. You'll learn ways to release controlling behavior, rather than trying to exert more control over yourself by using more willpower. Reading and practicing the interactive exercises included in this book will give you more trust in yourself, your body, mind, emotions, and Divine Spirit. Developing a deep level of self-confidence and trust is key to your weight balance success.

The eight myths from Chapter 1 and these three myths are worth noting because they are potentially dangerous in any combination. Why? Because when taken together, they collectively and progressively lead to more serious eating disorders, such as compulsive overeating, bulimia, and even anorexia, as well as long-term nutritional deficiencies.

Compulsive Overeaters, Bulimia, and Anorexia Defined

According to the National Eating Disorders Association, five to ten million women and girls and one million boys and men in the US suffer from some type of eating disorder. Many will die from serious complications arising from this behavior. Most people have no idea how dangerous this slippery slope can be in progressively leading to serious conditions that permanently undermine health.

Compulsive overeaters are those who continually overeat. There is no brain-stopping inner mechanism that communicates it is time to stop eating. Dinner could continue on into the evening with late-night snacks and even getting up to eat in the middle of the night. The word "compulsion" is used in the same way the word "addiction" can be used to describe this out-of-control type of eating.

Bulimia Nervosa is a serious eating disorder characterized by secret cycles of bingeing and purging. Bulimia nervosa can cause death. The three primary symptoms are (1) eating large amounts of food in a brief period of time, (2) feeling "out of control" and (3) an inability to feel fullness or hunger. Some kind of purging or a combination of the following usually follows eating binges: self-induced vomiting, laxative or diuretic use and abuse, fasting, and obsessive or compulsive exercise. Those afflicted with bulimia nervosa also possess a blown-out-of-proportion worry about body weight and shape. This condition is serious, yet treatable.

Anorexia Nervosa is a serious eating disorder characterized by self-starvation and excessive weight loss. Anorexia Nervosa can cause death. The five primary symptoms are as follows:

(1) rebelling against sustaining a bottom line normal weight for their height, age, activity level, or body build;
(2) extreme fear of weight gain;
(3) a prevalent fear of feeling fat, even when there is much weight loss;

(4) loss of menstrual periods in women and girls who have reached puberty; and

(5) extreme worries about body weight and shape.

Anorexia nervosa is most simply, self-starvation. It results in the highest death rates of all eating disorders.

The Difference between Dieting and More Serious Eating Disorders

What is the difference between dieting and bulimia? Bulimia Nervosa is all of the following:

- recurrent binge eating (rapid consumption of large amounts of food in a short period of time)
- feeling lack of control over eating behavior during a binge
- self-induced vomiting, use of laxatives or diuretics, strict dieting or fasting
- vigorous exercise in order to prevent weight gain
- and persistent concern with body shape and weight.

Please note that dieting and bulimic behavior *can* lead to anorexia.

In contrast, dieting is recurrent restriction of calories in order to lose weight. Usually dieting is followed by gradual or quick weight gain. Feelings of depression and other negative emotions are common to both Bulimia Nervosa and dieting. Simple dieting *can* progress to more serious eating disorders that affect brain function (depression) due to inadequate nutrition for extended periods of time.

When to Enlist the Help of a Therapist

When you have been unsuccessful using the exercises in this book, or are feeling blocked, defeated, totally hopeless or helpless, look for a therapist who specializes in eating disorders, *not* weight loss. A therapist who knows eating disorders is like a good coach who has the resources to pull together a winning team. Your body, mind, and spirit can be brought together to learn more balanced eating with the help of this professional.

What can you do to help a friend or loved one who is having dieting problems? Read as much as you can about eating disorders. Continue reading this book. Know the difference between fact and truth versus the myths about weight loss, diets, and exercise. Be honest and talk openly about your concerns with the person who is struggling with eating disorder or body image problems. Avoiding this subject or ignoring it completely is counterproductive. Be caring, but firm.

Mention the situation to someone else who cares about your friend. You can help by telling family, a counselor, teacher, or any other trusted adult. Remember that you can't force someone to change or to reach out for help, but you can share your honest concerns and the information you've found about where to find help. Ultimately, your friend needs to take responsibility and action for his or her problem and behavior.

Finding a Gentle Coach/Therapist to Show You the Long Term Way

It's scary just to think about finding a person whom you can trust with your innermost thoughts, doubts, and fears. Most of us don't want anyone to know these things about us. You may think, "I'd rather forget they ever happened." That's easy for you to say, but another thing to really do it. Those thoughts of the past are stored in the basement of your mind. When it gets too full these garbage thoughts start coming up the basement stairs. Then what do you do?

A person with an eating disorder will eat over it, starve over it, purge over it, over-exercise, but never really deal with it and get over it. Now is the time to discover a new way of handling it. The "stuff" we stuff can be a whole lot less scary when we decide to process and deal with it.

Have you heard the following spiritual axiom: "When the student is ready, the (spiritual) Master will appear"? Often the only prerequisite to this happening is hitting bottom. By hitting bottom I mean you get sick and tired of being sick and tired on every diet available. It's when you are ready to try anything that the advice and guidance of a skilled therapist who has experience in eating disorders or healthy eating can help you the most.

From my experience, here are a couple ways to find a therapist. Ask around among your friends and find out if they can recommend someone from personal experience. Another great idea is to call 800-931-2237 and ask for local therapist recommendations from NEDA. It's like a gift from heaven to find a therapist you can trust.

Forty-three Symptoms to Heed

The following questionnaire, *Self-Inventory for Dieting*, can be photocopied for multiple use. It will help you determine if you are suffering from a serious eating disorder or if you're experiencing any dieting symptoms you need to heed. You'll zero in on specific areas and chart how severe they are for you each time you take this inventory. It takes only two minutes to complete and is the first step to understanding what to do next.

Directions: Put a 0, 1, 2, or 3 in the space to the right of each symptom on the following list. Use the number that best describes how much each symptom upset you in the past week using the following scale: 0 – not at all, 1–sometimes, 2 – many times, 3 – most days.

You may take this inventory more often than once a week. If you take the test when you are feeling anxious or before or after an eating binge, make a note of this to the side of your results and write down whatever else was happening in your life. Take this inventory also when you're feeling at your best. By comparing the results during your best and worst times, you can get a better idea about your range of symptoms and the life events that trigger more symptoms.

Keep at least a weekly record of your progress while reading this book. Record and date your answers on a separate sheet of paper (numbered 1 to 43) in your journal, instead of using the spaces to the right of the list, if you choose.

Self Inventory for Dieting

Category 1: Dieting

_____ 1. *Do you have a problem with food?*

_____ 2. *How often do you binge?*

_____ 3. *Do you often make special trips to get binge foods?*

_____ 4. *Do you have special foods?*

_____ 5. *Do you feel urgency as you eat or binge?*

_____ 6. *Do you feel out of control when it is all gone?*

_____ 7. *Have you gained weight in the past year?*

_____ 8. *Do you exercise for longer than an hour per session or per day?*

_____ 9. *Do you try to control your binges?*

_____ 10. *Do you use pills or chemicals to stop yourself from bingeing?*

_____ 11. *Do any family members have what you would consider a food problem?*

_____ 12. *Do you think you have emotional problems?*

_____ 13. *Do family members think you have an emotional problem?*

_____ 14. *Have you ever considered suicide?*

_____ 15. *Did you seek professional help?*

_____ 16. *Does your relationship with food affect your job?*

_____ 17. *Does your relationship with food seem to affect your relationship with your boss?*

_____ 18. *Does your relationship with food seem to affect your relationship with family husband, boyfriend, mother, father, sister, brother, children)?*

_____ 19. *Does your relationship with food seem to affect your relationships with your friends?*

_____ 20. *When you're eating, do you find you want to be alone?*

_____ 21. *When you're eating, do you find you want to be with people?*

_____ 22. *When you're eating, do you find you want to be with people you trust?*

_____ 23. *When you're eating, do you find you want to be with strangers?*

_____ 24. *When you eat, do you find a quiet place?*

_____ 25. *When you eat, do you find a noisy place?*

_____ 26. *When you eat, do you find that the place doesn't matter?*

_____ 27. *Do you use laxatives?*

_____ 28. *Do you purge?*

_____ 29. *Do you purge more than once after a meal?*

_____ 30. *Do you ever use any medication to induce vomiting?*

_____ 31. *Have you ever had problems stopping the regurgitation effect?*

Category II Anxious Thoughts

___ 32. *Difficulty concentrating*
___ 33. *Fear of going crazy*
___ 34. *Fear of passing out*
___ 35. *Fear of being alone*
___ 36. *Fear of criticism or disapproval*

Category III Feelings

___ 37. *Feeling confused*
___ 38. *Feeling guilty and blaming yourself for everything*
___ 39. *Feeling weak and a loss of motivation*
___ 40. *Feeling angry*
___ 41. *Feeling hopeless*
___ 42. *Feeling helpless*
___ 43. *Feelings of hate for your body or behavior*

Add up your total score and record it:_____ Date:_____

Total score	What it means
0-5	No problem
5-12	Edging toward a problem
15-29	Mild problem
29-45	Medium problem
46-89	Severe problem
90-125	Extreme problem

How reliable is this inventory? If you track it weekly, look for a small change of one, two, or three points from week to week. This small change is a big step in your journey of feeling more balanced. Keeping track each week will help you learn to value and sustain each small step in building a new you. This inventory will help you chart your course to peace and balance.

Remember only you can choose to get better. Choose to monitor your progress as you read this book and do the exercises. As your totals go down, you make progress. Stay committed to the journey, even when your totals go up or stay the same. Keep saying to yourself until you believe it to the core of your being, "I choose to trust in positive outcomes."

To review:

1. Commit to singing your love song from Chapter 1 at the same time every day. Briefly record your experience in your journal.
2. Did you use feelings to describe your experience? Did you use thoughts to describe your experience? Did you describe how your body felt doing this? Rewrite again using feelings, thoughts, and body sensations.
3. Review the *Emotions Awareness Chart* and check off the emotions that you experience daily. At least once a week, write in your journal what greater truths your emotions brought to your awareness. Review your entries at least once a month to self-monitor your progress.
4. Take the *Self-Inventory for Dieting* at least once a week. Chart and review your totals at least once a month to see if certain life events trigger more symptoms. Strive to reduce your exposure to the stress of these events, when possible.

Now that you've gotten an understanding about diet cycles and gained some techniques for breaking the emotional traps that bind you, let's explore the power of asking the right questions to get the real answers you seek in the next chapter.

I'll also highlight books you can use as references to help you fashion a customized eating program which will give you optimum health and peak athletic performance while getting rid of food cravings, deprivation, and helping prevent and reverse disease. All this can be found in Chapter 4, as well as finding the inner resources you already possess to better channel your energies toward weight balance success.

Chapter 4
Asking the Right Questions

Freeing Yourself to Make Mistakes

The following story about Tina shows how making mistakes can work as wake-up calls to inspire a change for the better. When combined with awareness and asking the right questions, these mistakes can lead you to turn your life around.

Initially Tina sought help from a counselor for an eating disorder. "I'm here because of my weight and being so tired," Tina told the counselor. "This is a serious problem for me. I've gained 40 pounds, largely due to the fact that I can't sleep through the night. I get up and eat and then I'm so tired the next day that I can't work well. I can't stay awake in the evenings and I usually fall asleep at 8:00 p.m. each night."

The counselor asked Tina many questions and found she was depressed and had repeated thoughts of her husband dying. Tina told the counselor that each time she came home from work, she binged on snack foods and couldn't stop until she went to sleep. She found all of this was causing her to become more distant from her husband. She and her husband both wanted her to get these issues addressed, and it was her husband who suggested that she seek treatment under his HMO plan.

The counselor thought about Tina's problems and how she could address them under the guidelines of the HMO plan before recommending that Tina see a psychiatrist to get evaluated for medication.

"If you are experiencing tiredness, sleeplessness, weight gain, anxiety, and repeated thoughts of your husband's death," she said gently, "I'm sure a psychiatrist can work with you to relieve the depression and insomnia."

"That would be great," Tina said with relief as she agreed.

The psychiatrist in Tina's HMO plan was an hour away, so Tina had to see him on her only day off. It took numerous calls for Tina to set up an appointment with him; then the doctor canceled her first appointment after she had arrived at his office. It took another four weeks before Tina could see him. Initially he started her on a single medication.

Tina kept seeing her counselor during this time. The medication from the psychiatrist gave her more energy, however her sexual interest and sexual feelings went numb. This disturbed Tina since this was the one area of her life that she hadn't had problems with previously. Needless to say, Tina wasn't happy with the medication.

After two weeks she returned to the doctor and told him about the loss of sexual feelings. "The medications still aren't helping me sleep. I still wake up several times a night."

"Here's another prescription plus an additional one which will help you sleep," said the doctor. Tina hesitated, but said, "OK."

"Take these two new medications with what you're already taking for the next two weeks, then come back to see me," he said.

Tina took the combined medications, but they were a hassle. Each day Tina came home from work, she fell asleep on the couch by 6:00 p.m., and yet still awoke at 3:00 a.m. She could hardly finish her work the next day due to being groggy and tired. This didn't make sense to her because these were the issues she was paying the doctor to address. On top of everything else, her sexual interest disappeared completely. This was most disturbing to her and her husband.

The next time Tina went to the doctor, she mentioned the grogginess, tiredness, falling asleep early, not sleeping through the night, and the complete loss of sexual feelings. "The medications make me groggy during the day. They don't seem to help," she said.

"Here, try this prescription instead. Also, these will help you sleep. Remember it takes time for your body to adjust. Come back and see me in three weeks," he said.

Tina wanted to tell the doctor what she thought of the medications but held back, figuring she needed to give the doctor's advice a little more time. She hesitantly filled the prescriptions, then went home and started taking the new medications.

From this point on, her life was a mess. She looked terrible and every time she took the medications she felt worse than ever. Her husband was worried. He tried talking to Tina, but she was so groggy that she couldn't listen. Her husband took time off from work one afternoon to cuddle and be romantic with Tina, but nothing happened. It was the worst situation Tina could imagine.

After more than three months of prescription changes, Tina had a shelf full of pills and was no closer to a good night's sleep. She talked to her counselor and told her that she'd had it. "I've never taken medications before, and now I have three prescriptions I take twice a day. When I showed up for my last appointment, the doctor's office was locked so I went home and called.

"The receptionist who answered the phone rudely asked, 'Didn't you get the message that the office is moving? Well, there was a sign in the window.'" She told Tina that the doctor's office would call to set up another appointment. That was two weeks ago and Tina hadn't heard from them since.

Tina steamed with frustration and anger as she talked to the counselor. Eventually, Tina concluded that she wanted to wean herself off the medications since they only caused more complications and sexual dysfunction.

A week later she returned to her counselor and said, "You know, I am much happier off the medications. I feel alive."

"I am happy to hear this," the counselor said. Tina and the counselor continued their work on Tina's underlying feelings of guilt that had led to the bingeing and depression in the first place. Tina was pleased and relieved with what she had learned. She returned home and reconnected with her husband.

From that moment on, Tina and her husband became allies, working together to ask the right questions. Eventually they discovered through the Internet that Chronic Fatigue Syndrome (CFS) is often misdiagnosed as depression. Tina's husband saw the information first and said, "This sounds like you, Tina."

They found dietary and supplement recommendations for CFS from books at the local library as well as Web sites dedicated to CFS on the Internet. When Tina applied the suggestions for dietary and lifestyle changes, her health improved.

Tina and her husband discovered through this experience that they were relieved to be free of the side effects from the medications. Subsequently they developed a stronger commitment to living more balanced in every aspect of their lives. Through Tina's determination to ask the right questions and practice awareness, she addressed the underlying cause of her tiredness as CFS and treated it at the source. With proper diet, nutritional supplements, lifestyle changes and time, Tina eventually alleviated all her symptoms and gained true permanent weight balance. Ultimately Tina felt better for having made the journey— and survived the worst it could get.

Leave No Stone Unturned in Your Quest

One resource that is often overlooked in the search for weight balance success is a thorough check-up by your family intern or general physician. A complete physical examination and full blood work done by your physician or a qualified nutritionist who knows what to look for can often isolate developing underlying medical conditions that can potentially cause unexpected weight gain (CFS, fibromyalgia, diabetes, and arthritis, to name only a few).

Some other possible causes of weight gain are head injuries, food allergies and sensitivities, candidiasis, thyroid conditions, hormonal imbalances, as well as interactions between herbs, over-the-counter and/or prescription drugs and medications, or cortisone (steroid) drugs.

In *The Food Allergy Cure*, Ellen Cutler writes, "Reports of food allergies began to appear in Europe in the early 1900s, and since the 1940s these allergies have been recognized by doctors around the world. Doctors estimate that up to two million people in the United States are affected by food allergies."

The symptoms allergies present include the following: hives, eczema, asthma, gastrointestinal disturbances (diarrhea, cramping, nausea, swelling, gas, even colitis), headaches, migraines, attention deficit hyperactivity disorder, cold and canker sores, recurrent ear infections, arthritis pain, fatigue, premenstrual and menopausal symptoms, infertility, *obesity, bulimia and other eating disorders*. Other medical reasons may cause these complaints; however Cutler says if you have already explored these possibilities and your physician cannot explain the symptoms, your might consider being tested for food allergies. Some of the most likely culprits for food allergies are refined carbohydrates (pasta, breads, and pastries), chocolate, and sugar, among others.

Cutler has developed a protocol, outlined in *The Food Allergy Cure*, that clears allergies from your system. It's a comprehensive approach for retiring allergies and the food cravings, weight gain, and depression that often accompany them--for good. This book is worth checking out if you suspect that you have allergies or food sensitivities.

A Most Important Tool for Regulating Weight Balance

> *A change in eating habits, patterns, and foods can always dramatically affect weight gain at any age.*

It's appropriate to look at whether you're getting the right foods (macronutrients) in the proper ratios for your metabolic type. One of the most powerful tools for regulating your body's ability to metabolize food is proper nourishment—basically food choices geared to your individual needs.

Isolating the root cause of what accelerated the weight gain in the first place and treating the originating offender is often the first step to reversing obesity. When you combine this tactic with eating a diet that's perfectly attuned for you metabolically and getting proper exercise, you'll attain steady, lasting results in your quest for weight balance success.

A Crucial Reference for Weight Balance Success

The most important weight balance tool you'll need is a comprehensive guide to nutrition and the proper foods. This guide can serve as a foundation resource for your eating patterns for the rest of your life. *The Metabolic Typing Diet* by William L. Wolcott with Trish Fahey, is by far the best system I've found for customizing food to your individual nutritional needs.

This definitive work is based on more than seventy years of comprehensive research, pioneering effort, and discoveries from various physicians, biochemists, dentists, physiologists, clinical nutritionists, and psychologists. Its dynamic, groundbreaking technology teaches you how to metabolically fine-tune your diet to meet your unique nutritional needs.

Providing you with the tools to understand, address, and speed up your metabolism through the foods you eat is only the first step. Metabolic typing also gives you the ability and flexibility to adjust your diet with great precision and accuracy as your metabolism shifts throughout your life. You can achieve and maintain your ideal weight with no feelings of deprivation and be free of food cravings and hunger forever with this cutting edge approach. This simple, user-friendly book is the last one you'll need on how to eat well to stay well. It boosts your immune system, naturally conquers indigestion and fatigue, prevents and reverses chronic illness while helping you overcome depression, anxiety, and mood swings. Metabolic typing is considered the "missing link" in modern nutrition science today.

Your quest for weight balance begins when you integrate and synchronize the truth about food from *The Metabolic Typing Diet* with the techniques, exercises, and visualizations in this book. Take the Metabolic Type Self-Test on page 135 of *The Metabolic Typing Diet*, start applying its principles, and you'll begin feeling and looking better today.

Another must-have book for your personal reference is Julia Ross' *The Diet Cure*, which offers specific recommendations to natural supplements that will supply your brain with nutrients needed to eliminate food cravings, depression, low energy, anxiety, and sleeplessness. Ross also lists interventions for other physical problems and gives step-by-step solutions. Be sure to check out the Amino Acid Therapy Chart for balancing brain chemistry in her book.

Cut a Striking Figure and Look Thinner

When many people are asked why they want to be thinner, three reasons come up often. They are (1) to be healthier, (2) to be more physically active throughout life and (3) to look better in clothes. Granted, being thinner doesn't necessarily guarantee being healthier or more physically active, but looking better in your clothes can begin right now, even *before you lose a single pound!*

In *Flatter Your Figure,* Jan Larkey shares a fun way to "figure out your figure" which uses no measuring tapes—just two sticks, a string, and a friend. Not only does she help you discern why some clothes look great on you while others make you look 10 pounds heavier, her style guide helps you find the most flattering styles—and pinpoints which ones to avoid for your specific figure challenges.

Camouflaging figure problems is only the first step to looking the best you can be, according to Larkey. Her book covers everything from basics to accessories. It explores how to use fabrics and prints and gives special strategies for appearing thinner or taller. *Flatter Your Figure* is a personalized guide for women to coordinate the most flattering ensembles from their wardrobes. This system engenders the utmost confidence in knowing that your figure assets are accented always.

How you look in clothes also depends on getting the best fit and the right size. On page 9 of *Fitting Finesse* by Nancy Zieman is a method for determining your correct size by taking one simple measurement—your front width measurement. Zieman includes a front width fitting chart and complete detailed directions for getting an accurate measurement. (Ask a friend to help you with this).

Zieman notes, "You may be pleasantly surprised by the results of the front width measurement. It is very common for someone who has been sewing with a size 20 in order to fit her bust to find out she is actually a size 16."

Although *Fitting Finesse* is written primarily for home sewers, Zieman's recommendations for measuring your figure will help you determine the right size and right area of the store in which to shop the next time you're looking for clothes. Her additional trouble-shooting methods and tips for sizing up the tailoring will come in handy when you're checking the quality of your potential buys in the fitting room as well.

Height and Weight Proportionate

A better determinant of your ability to maintain health and remain physically active throughout your life is finding out if your height and weight are balanced in proportion to each other. Have you heard of BMI (Body Mass Index)?

Body Mass Index specifically relates your height in proportion to your weight. Many BMI calculators can be accessed on the World Wide Web through your favorite search engine. One such online calculator is at http://cc.ysu.edu/~doug/hwp.cgi.

First type in your height in inches and your weight in pounds. Then click on "calculate." This body mass calculation is based on the ratio of weight (in kilograms or pounds) to height (in meters or inches) squared. For **most** people, this number falls between 20 and 25.

The calculator not only gives you a body mass ratio number for your current weight to height, it also provides a zone of weight for your height. If your ratio is far less than 20 or far greater than 25, a bit of weight balancing by using this book and *The Metabolic Typing Diet* can help you move closer to an ideal zone.

Please note that the BMI range can give you a ballpark of weights that *might* be best for you—in other words, those that can help provide optimal health and strength to personal weight—but do take the BMI calculator with a grain of salt. Since it does not measure body fat and does not take into consideration activity levels, life styles, and healthy eating patterns, as a measure of obesity and overweight, it *can* be flawed.

Instead of trying to hold your weight too firmly to it, use it as a general rule that can be helpful for gauging the ballpark. The cut-off points can be arbitrary, because if your weight is above the 25 - 29.9, you can still be in a range that is normal and healthy for your individual metabolism. According to Glenn Gaesser, Ph.D., weight levels above these are *not* unhealthy when you practice a regular exercise routine and eat a healthy, balanced diet.

Those who have been overweight and sedentary since a young age may need to start slowly with the exercises recommended in Chapter 4 to bust *Myth #2: Exercise More and Lose Weight.*

One additional element to take into consideration when fine-tuning the weight balance estimate that's right for you is a basic test to determine whether you have a small, medium, or large bone structure.

Measuring Your Bone Structure

Encircle the bony part of your wrist with the longest finger and thumb of your other hand. If your finger and thumb overlap, you're small-boned. If they just meet, your medium-boned. If they don't meet at all at the boniest circumference of your wrist, you're most likely large-boned.

Establishing Realistic Goals

Big-boned people feel healthier and stronger at heavier weights than small-boned people of the same height do. In addition, men are healthier at heavier weights than women of the same height mostly because of muscle mass (since men are generally more highly muscled than women are).

Muscle weighs more than fat, so it makes sense that anyone (male or female) who is well-muscled will be healthier (as well as more fit) at a heavier weight. Muscle also burns fat, so developing more muscle increases your fat-burning capacity.

The right weight for you is a judgment call you can make based on your personal observations about yourself and what you know feels best for you. Please try to take every personal factor (including age) into consideration when determining your best balanced weight and be sure to practice understanding, compassion, and benevolence with yourself.

One quick note: It is generally agreed that carrying extra weight around your abdominal area is a sign of more serious health concerns. If your waist measurement is about ten inches less than your chest/bust measurement, you're in the healthy zone. When your waist measurement starts to inch toward equaling or exceeding your chest/bust measurement, it's time to take immediate steps toward a healthier diet and weight balance, ideally using *The Metabolic Typing Diet.*

Learning How to Ask the Right Questions to Get Answers

After you read and apply the principles in *The Metabolic Typing Diet,* you'll want to further develop your ability to ask the right questions. Be aware that the answers can come from many places. Within every question is an answer waiting to be discovered.

When Carol stumbled upon this concept, she began asking questions right and left. Some of her favorite questions evolved out of her goal statement of "I want to lose weight." She turned this statement into a series of positive questions such as, "How do I learn to eat in a balanced way to maintain my desired weight?" Carol chose questions that began with the words what, where, and when, such as, "What is balanced eating?" and "Where do I find the support I need to maintain more balanced eating?" Carol let her mind follow the clues generated by these questions, similar to following clues in a mystery. Carol found the answers she sought in the library, at the bookstore, at a local health center, and even through the Yellow Pages.

Carol decided to have some fun, so she called whomever she thought would have the answers from the listings in the Yellow Pages. Some people were helpful; others weren't. Carol ended up with notes and more phone numbers to call. She picked a good day to follow the trail to answers. She expected it to be an unexpected adventure and it was! Carol found four personal trainers near her home and one nutritionist that day. She was able to make appointments to interview them later that week.

Harnessing the Power of Your Dreams

Another way to get answers is to ask questions in a dream as illustrated in the next story. Toni, a woman struggling to lose weight, had a dream where she met a famous diet authority as he lectured in a mall. Toni stopped to listen and asked him, "How do I lose weight?"

The answer she received was, "It must be from the inside out." This answer came from her Higher Power through her inner wisdom and it pulled at her heartstrings for it meant a lot to her. On one hand, Toni wanted to lose weight; on the other hand, she was pulled by what she loved to eat. What decision would she make? To gain the result she wanted, Toni needed to decide what to release from her life. Those of us who want to lose weight need to ask positively turned questions that will ensure balance.

Even when using an excellent resource such as *The Metabolic Typing Diet*, initially we may be pulled by food cravings because we've built a dependence upon them or we are allergic to them. We need to ask ourselves, "What do I need to keep in my food plan and what needs to be released?"

Foods Can Be Your Best Friends

Foods can rejuvenate and help shape your body. In *The Metabolic Typing Diet*, turn to the list of foods that are right for your metabolic type. Here's a fun, healthy foods exercise.

Find a quiet time and a quiet place. Close your eyes and remember a time from long ago when you felt wonderful and excited. Take your time with this. Remember what you were seeing or experiencing. Remember your feelings of excitement, openness, how energized you were with youthful energy and adventure. Let these feelings fill your heart.

Now open your eyes and switch your attention to the list of foods that are right for you. Still embracing your feelings of excitement, openness, and adventure, ask which ones you would be willing to include more of in your lifestyle. Marrying your feelings to your intentions may entice better eating habits, which lead to a more shapely body and better health for you.

A Helpful Natural Aid for Weight Balance, Enhanced Mood, and Sleep

If you're accustomed to a diet based largely on refined carbohydrates, fruits, and sugars with very little emphasis on protein or fat, chances are you may be unconsciously using food to stimulate serotonin production in your brain (in an attempt to use food to make you feel good).

Abusing your body by eating refined carbohydrates and sugars without the proper balance of vegetables, proteins and fats can seriously compromise your health and bring on diabetic and pre-diabetic conditions with time. It is also predominantly responsible for weight gain due to increasing fat reserves.

This type of eating pattern is also subconsciously addictive. It's relatively easy to become addicted to your own body chemicals (serotonin, adrenaline, among others) and subconsciously repeat certain behavior patterns, such as binge eating of refined carbohydrates, in order to stimulate serotonin production. Anyone who has eschewed a balanced diet in favor of one based largely upon sugars and refined carbohydrates is familiar with the food "high" or "rush" that can result.

You can address your serotonin needs without resorting to stressing your body by abusing food. Simply take 50 to 100 milligrams of 5-Hydroxytryptophan (5-HTP)—an over-the-counter amino acid—once a day to elevate your serotonin levels without compromising your eating habits.

This essential amino acid is a common building block for proteins. An ordinary food source of 5-HTP is Thanksgiving turkey dinner. Most people consume much more than 100 milligrams of this amino acid then (proving its safety and lack of harmful side effects). Not only does 5-HTP help to elevate mood, it aids weight balance, and helps supply a good night's sleep.

You can break the vicious cycle of bingeing on carbohydrates and sugars while addressing your serotonin needs by adding a high quality form of 5-HTP to your morning supplements.

Some high quality brands of 5-Hydroxytryptophan are from Thorne Research and Ultra Pure by Life Link. These can be found either through a reputable health care practitioner or ordered from your local health food store.

Pause and re-read the story of Tina. Use the resources of *The Metabolic Typing Diet, Flatter Your Figure, Fitting Finesse,* and *The Mood Cure* to better understand where you're at and start feeling better about where you're going. Review the exercise that Carol used to find the answers she needed with her questions. See if you can think of some questions and begin opening yourself up to discovering the answers as they appear in your life this week. This is fun and surprising.

The next chapter covers more on how to connect your intuitive side with your feelings through inner exercises. When you safely explore the rich fertile ground of dealing with your feelings, you're on the way to having your life blossom in ways you've always wanted.

Chapter 5
Dealing with Feelings

Identifying Hidden Feelings So You Can Take Positive Action

> *Remember your feelings are a golden key in your quest for weight balance freedom.*

By now you've been checking your feelings every evening. If you've neglected to do this, use this as a gentle reminder to begin checking in with your feelings daily. When you feel guilt, strive to find the truth underneath that guilt. If you find anger comes up and you've never dealt with it before except by bingeing, find the deeper truth your intuitive self is trying to tell you.

The technique of getting in touch with your emotions is similar to healing an infection. An adhesive covering an infection just won't heal it. The infection needs to come to the surface and be addressed, so that the wound can heal from the inside out.

To cover it over is similar to stuffing feelings. Ignored and stuffed feelings create an infection in your subconscious. Eventually those stuffed feelings have to surface and be healed in appropriate ways. If not, they build up as ever-present subconscious stresses that cause major imbalances in your health, which eventually manifest as heart disease, cancer, and other serious diseases.

The following chart is *The Graduate Level Feeling Chart.* You can make copies of it to use for several weeks. Put a check mark by each feeling that you experience during the day. No second guessing or changing your first impression; the first hint or nudge is the honest truth for you. If you haven't made a habit of knowing your feelings, then you need to go back and do the exercise in Chapter 2 until you can recognize your true feelings.

Remember feelings aren't good or bad; they are just feelings. Do this exercise because you choose to show yourself love and take the best care of yourself that you can for now. You will benefit from this for the rest of your life.

Graduate Level Feeling Chart

	Monday	Tuesday	Wednesday	Thursday	Friday	Saturday	Sunday
Annoyed							
Fiery							
Fuming							
Rejected							
Embarrassed							
Confused							
Frustrated							
Sarcastic							
Disappointed							
Used/Abused							
Burdened							
Discouraged							
Self-punishing							
Bitter							
Hurt							
Attacked							
Adaptable							
Open							
Caring							
Amused							
Attractive							
Numb							
Involved							
Questioned							
Safe							
At peace							
Opposing							
Bothered							
Indignant							
Choosy							
Optimistic							

| Deserving |
| Approachable |
| Acceptable |

Graduate Level Feeling Chart (*continued*)

	Monday	Tuesday	Wednesday	Thursday	Friday	Saturday	Sunday
Hateful							
Worthy							
Overwrought							
Seething							
Belligerent							
Furious							
Hysterical							
Prepared							
Encouraging							
Invigorated							
Adequate							
Answerable							
Refreshed							
Aware							
Wounded							
Unappreciated							
Dumb							
Offended							
Fascinated							
Needed							
Understanding							
Essential							
Tuned-in							
Welcome							
Appreciated							
Trapped							
Put upon							
Deprived							
Vindictive							
Picked upon							

Withholding
Admirable
Delighted
Alive
Jubilant

Graduate Level Feeling Chart (continued)

	Monday	Tuesday	Wednesday	Thursday	Friday	Saturday	Sunday
Excited							
Trusting							
Let down							
Threatened							
Frightened							
Ignored							
Overlooked							
Unwelcome							
Brave							
Affectionate							
Daring							
Bold							
Considered							
Proud							
Betrayed							
Defeated							
Unacceptable							
Despondent							
Ruined							
Lucky							
Reliable							
Sincere							
Purposeful							
Concerned							
Productive							
Pessimistic							
Rigid							

Stagnant	
Destructive	
Immobilized	
Unfeeling	
Disconnected	
Attuned with	
In balance	

Graduate Level Feeling Chart (continued)

	Monday	Tuesday	Wednesday	Thursday	Friday	Saturday	Sunday
Tender							
Congruent							
Creative							
Appreciative							
Gentle							
Neglected							
Unimportant							
Morbid							
Unloved							
Melancholy							
Deserted							
Quiet							
Unified							
Fulfilled							
Completed							
Connected							
At one							
Perceptive							

A Word about Perceiving and Judging Your Feelings

How you were taught to perceive and judge your feelings when you were growing up is what stops you from feeling and acknowledging the truth beneath those feelings right now. It is normal and human to experience many feelings throughout the day. What you want to learn from the practice of charting your feelings are ways to clear or process all feelings, so that you don't continued to carry them around in the background any more.

For example, if you don't seem to experience anger ever, this is a red flag warning you that you're in deep denial about your anger. Getting to the truth at the root of your anger is a key to being free of it.

The best time to chart your emotions is at the end of the day. If you continually find you're stuck in the same emotional bandwidth, ask yourself the following questions and write the answers to them in your journal. These questions will help you get clear about the facts regarding your emotions and feelings. The answers to these questions will help you reach freedom and balance eventually.

Journal Questions to Ask When You're Stuck in Your Emotions

Remember when you do this questioning part of the exercise, you need to make the effort and be persistent. Results will follow.

Question 1: What are my thoughts in connection to this feeling?
Question 2: What did I think next? How did I feel about it?

Keep asking the above questions and write down as many answers as you get, boiling it down for as long as it takes, until you get to the bottom where there are no more thoughts and no more feelings.

Drawing Can Uncover What's Hidden for You

Next draw a stick figure or something else that represents where you are after the last question. Put a dialogue balloon over its head and let the drawing speak to you. What would it say if you drew anything else?

Write three sentences that begin with, "I am _____" underneath the picture and finish the sentence with a different characteristic of what you felt when you drew the picture.

Remember to do the best you can. There is no right or wrong way to do this drawing. The important thing is to take action and do it. When you draw, use symbols and images—the easiest language for the subconscious to understand. This exercise is valuable in beginning to clear out feelings that are blocking you.

After you do this exercise, wait a few minutes and see if you start feeling better. Then check again later in the day to see if the feelings have decreased in intensity. Learn to look for shifts and little steps that will lead you to feeling better. You'll find as you check in with your feelings, you'll learn which ones lead to overeating, bingeing, starving or other compulsive eating behaviors. Acknowledging unconscious habits and fear of feelings, rather than denying them, puts you on your way to balancing them and finding out what will truly make you happy. Feelings are the key to your truth.

What to Expect When You First Begin to Chart Your Feelings

In the beginning, recognize that it's okay to feel safe about acknowledging your feelings. It is equally okay to feel disheartened when you first start to practice checking your feelings daily. These feelings need to come up in your awareness because they have been hiding too long in your subconscious where they have been causing trouble. Any discomfort you experience will pass as you continue to do the freeing techniques in this book.

Freeing Hidden Emotions So You Can Take Positive Action

As you begin to ask for answers in your life, you'll encounter truth when you are ready. Working with hidden emotions can be difficult only because they haven't been dealt with before. The frustrations, anxiety, fearful and out-of-control feelings seem overwhelming, but the more you deal with them, the less difficult they will become until they loosen their hold on you. So how do you muster up the initial courage and approach this process with an adventurous spirit?

Connecting with Your Adventurous Spirit

The way to connect to an adventurous spirit is to first define what this state of mind orconsciousness is for you. In other words, where is your attention? How do you feel in your attitude toward your quest? Remember the three keys of attitude, attention, and mechanics when tapping into your adventurous spirit.

A woman named Sherry illustrated how she used these three keys to unlock her adventurous spirit. First she practiced an imaginative technique. Then she used her attention and imagination to complete the exercise, and finally she used an observer attitude in viewing herself doing the technique. The observer attitude comes from Soul, your true Self. This attitude will feel neutral and balanced. You can enhance the observer attitude by invoking a sense of anticipation, as if toward an adventure that is about to begin, heightening the fun.

Here's what Sherry did: she started by closing her eyes and gently focusing on the imaginary spot in the center of her forehead where insight occurs in the brain. Then silently she asked her Higher Power to connect her to her hidden feelings. Next, she imagined walking in a beautiful, shady garden bordered by low granite walls and lacy wrought-iron gates.

As Sherry walked the stone path through the garden, she noticed a huge weed growing in the middle of the walkway. She bent down and began to pull it up. The first part of it, composed of many small roots, came up easily. But Sherry was surprised to find that there was a single, long taproot holding it in. She pulled with all her strength, pulling and pulling until the root let go.

Then she asked her Higher Power if this huge weed-like plant was poisonous. When she found that it *was*, she asked if she could transplant it in her garden and watch it change positively.

Sherry found just the right place for the weed. As she transplanted it, she began to notice that it changed into something beautiful. She watched closely as its breathtaking beauty blossomed before her eyes.

You can try this technique, too. It makes you aware of any weed-like feelings you might have in the garden of your consciousness. It sets up an adventure consciousness similar to that of going on a vacation when you are excited and looking at everything in a new way. Try this imaginative exercise every night before you go to sleep, or in the morning just before your day begins. Set one time a day to do this routine. You'll be surprised at the results.

When you assume a goal of finding hidden feelings that have blocked you from taking positive action in the past, you can be assured that you'll find symbols of those feelings in your visualizations. Acting as if you have the means to deal with these images in symbolic ways paves the way for you to achieve this goal. In this case, setting up a regular time to practice the above technique works gradually on a subconscious level to free your life from the unconscious emotions that strive to stay hidden.

Taking the Technique One Step Further

Sherry went further in the exercise by asking, "What does pulling up the taproot mean to my process?" Upon further reflection, Sherry discovered the meaning of what pulling up the taproot meant for her: it was pulling out hidden, buried resentments toward the men in her life. These resentments had affected balance in her life with regard to eating.

In the past when she interacted with men, Sherry felt overwhelmed. A few hours later, she would binge on muffins or jelly beans. Sherry discovered that by doing this technique she was pulling up her resentments towards men and inviting them to transform. The more she practiced the visualization, the less overwhelmed she was around men. Sherry became more aware of when she began to feel resentments in the moment and was able to calm herself by taking charge of her response and affecting the outcome of these interactions. Her muffin/jelly bean binges decreased with this change and she was on her way to being totally free of the binges.

Writing and Drawing Can Uncover What's Hidden from You

Put your attention on an area of your life and let the inner conflicts it elicits pop into your awareness. This could be anything about which you've had mixed feelings. Next, write the feelings down. Use "I-feel statements" such as "I feel confused," or "I feel anxious, afraid, sad, out of control" because these statements will help you take ownership and responsibility for your feelings. You can check your *Graduate Level Feeling Chart* to find out which emotions recur for you most often and use them. Chronicle them here or in your journal.

I feel _____

_____

_____

_____

_____

Now draw a doodle picture of those feelings in your journal. You can pretend that you don't know how to draw even if you do. This attitude helps free your Spirit of Childhood to experiment and have fun. Then draw a funny stick doodle figure of your feelings. You can use a dialogue balloon above its head and write what the figure might want to say.

Next make a positive change in the picture or in what it wants to release. This technique works every time to uncover hidden feelings. It is enough to experience the feelings in this way for now. Feeling your emotions, recognizing them, then taking some action on those emotions will help you let them go.

Forming a Deeper Connection to Move through Your Emotions and Fears

In the next story, Sherry used an exercise to help her form a deeper connection to her feelings in order to move through them and past her fears. She used it as a way to resolve a long-standing challenge that she'd never been able to face, let alone begin to address.

Sherry had been working on several aspects of her process. However, one challenge remained for her—the challenge of encountering the void.

Sherry described the void as complete vulnerability, which left her so helpless and without hope that she felt terror and thoughts of death. Sherry would be stuck in panic while in this emotional state.

As a child, Sherry had continual nightmares and she would hide under the covers. At this point, Sherry recognized that this void was part of her fear of abandonment. A completely helpless feeling that no one was there for her would overcome her. Although she had asked her Higher Power many times to clear this black void and the intense irritation that she experienced when she got close to someone she cared about, Sherry had no idea how to approach the process of resolving it. This was because on the other side of her defenses was an inner wall.

Then one night her Higher Power gave Sherry a dream. She wrote the dream down as soon as she awoke. Then she went back into the dream and used imagination and visualization to address and resolve her fear of the void (abandonment). This is what she wrote:

"I went back into the dream in my imagination and just watched. Soon I remembered that I was standing behind a chain link fence. I moved towards the house and opened the gate in the fence. As I looked at the house, I knew I was walking to the house of my Higher Power—God's house. The door was wide open with warm light streaming out. I began clearing my emotions.

"Mostly what I felt was overwhelming fear. I could hear myself saying, 'You can do it. You are always safe.' I used every effort of inner strength to step up on the first step of the stairway that led to the open door.

"Next I felt like I had to move through an iron wall, just to step into the doorway. I entered and was catapulted into the void into blackness, helplessness, terror, and complete vulnerability.

"Then I sensed the soft whispers, the Voice of my Higher Power telling me what to do. I listened. I sensed my inner ears hearing these words, 'Trust that you are loved as you allow the blackness to engulf you. Just be, and know that in being, you are love.' This experience of being aware that I was love eliminated the illusion of blackness and the void."

Sherry wrote how powerfully loving this experience was and how she felt uplifted for weeks later. That experience is part of her consciousness forever.

Try this exercise of going back into a dream with the help of your Higher Power. If experiences don't happen for you right away, try again. You may have to spend time playing at it. Sometimes you will meet your Higher Power in disguise on a street in your dreams. You will know this by a feeling of upliftment or love that accompanies the experience. You'll either feel lightness or joy when you are with your Higher Power, or when the experience is over. The upliftment and joy is a blessing given to you in divine love.

The Hidden Answers within Three Steps

1. Keep writing in your journal, asking questions to your Higher Power like, "What is my next step?" Chronicle the answers you receive.
2. Contemplate and pray as you connect to your Higher Power.
3. Taking courageous new actions out of compassion and true inner self-love once the foundation is set.

A Technique for Finding Answers in Your Dreams

1. *Before you go to sleep, write down in your journal a question for which you would like an answer. Ask to receive a dream with the answer in it, in a way you cannot possibly misunderstand. Keep your journal and a pen beside your bed.*
2. *Before you go to sleep, read your question over ten times with a strong feeling of love.*
3. *Be ready to write down your dream and the answers within it immediately upon awakening.*

To review:

1. Commit to singing your love song to yourself each day at the same time daily.
2. Get a physical examination and complete blood work if you think it's necessary and check out *The Metabolic Typing Diet* by William L. Wolcott with Trish Fahey and *The Mood Cure* by Julia Ross.
3. Ask and write down questions that arise naturally from your goal statement and go on an adventure to find the answers. Check out the wisdom contained in your local library, on the Internet, local bookstores, health food stores, and health centers and other businesses found in the Yellow Pages.
4. Use *The Graduate Level Feeling Chart* daily and journal the answers to the following questions when you become stuck in emotions:

Question 1: What are my thoughts in connection to this feeling?

Question 2: What did I think next? How did I feel about it?

5. Use the drawing exercise to uncover and release blockages from hidden emotions.
6. Remember to use the three keys of attitude, attention, and mechanics when connecting with your Higher Power during visualizations and dreams.

7. Practice the *Hidden Answers within Three Steps* exercise and *The Technique for Finding Answers in Dreams.* Write the results in your journal.

In Chapter 6, we'll explore successful techniques for getting unstuck emotionally and verbally, and discover more on how to process anger and other strong emotions.

Chapter 6
Getting Unstuck and Saying NO

Tips for Getting Unstuck and Moving Beyond Discouragement

Sherry has made excellent progress so far. After several sessions, she's recognized that she subconsciously relies upon the myths of "Dieting Will Make Others Proud of Me" and "Dieting Will Make My World All Right."

> *She has also uncovered her deeper truth behind this myth, which is the human need for love.*

Sherry made her positive purpose statement (*I am on my way to being successful through learning the secrets to weight balance success*) and chose a personal symbol that represents her success (a star), which she uses in visualizations every day. Sherry also incorporated the Five-plus Passkeys to Success (setting up her environment for success, committing herself to new behaviors and self-monitoring them).

In her session last week, Sherry asked, "What changes can I make to jump-start my weight balance success and resolve my fears?" She's begun applying principles from *The Metabolic Typing Diet* and started changing her eating habits and patterns. She also utilized some of the techniques, exercises, and visualizations offered in Chapter 4.

When Sherry enters the room this week, I notice she's feeling defeated. Her body language loudly broadcasts discouragement as she slumps into a chair. As we talk, Sherry's hands twist nervously and she looks down at the floor. She expresses disappointment about not losing as much weight as fast as she wanted.

"I just can't seem to lose any weight," she says. "I'm doing all the right things, such as balancing my carbohydrates, proteins and fats according to the Metabolic Typing Diet. I'm eating the right *kinds* of carbohydrates and three balanced meals a day without bingeing." She sighs as I listen.

"You didn't lose a *single* pound this week?" I ask for clarification.

Sherry paused to reflect. "Well, I did lose a couple, but my secretary lost six pounds the first week she started her diet. This week I only lost two!"

"I understand," I said. "You sound discouraged. But a better indicator would be to evaluate your energy level and note how well your clothes are fitting."

"My energy level *is* good," Sherry admitted, "and my clothes *are* much more comfortable."

"It sounds like you might be leaning toward buying into the myth of eating less to lose weight, but I think you already know where that will lead. If you stay on track and continue with your metabolic plan, I think you'll soon begin to see much more weight balance success. By the way, did you know the discouragement you're feeling right now is a positive sign?" I ask.

"It *is?*" Sherry responds, incredulously.

"It's an indicator that we need to take different measures and be even more creative with techniques, exercises and visualizations to help you break through this bog of emotions. We need to do further fine-tuning to achieve your target. What would be more helpful for your attitude right now is to choose to trust in positive outcomes."

Sherry sighs and slumps a little more as she looks at the floor. I can tell she's gotten herself into an emotional quagmire that's hard to shake.

"How are you feeling emotionally right now?" I ask.

"I feel like a failure," Sherry says. "I'm scared, pessimistic, unacceptable, and frustrated. And I feel awful that I didn't do as well as my secretary."

I suggest to Sherry that she visualize what feelings of discouragement look like. Notice I said to focus on *feelings* of discouragement, not the *thought* that she's a failure.

"What would discouragement look like to you?" I ask Sherry. "Imagine a picture of your PAST discouragement." Since the subconscious mind doesn't differentiate between past and present, I verbally emphasize the word *past.* In this way, I'm encouraging Sherry to move through this stage as quickly as possible and put it *in the past.*

I ask, "Does your past discouragement look like a sunny field of wild flowers?"

"No! It looks more like a dark warehouse. Everything is empty blackness." Sherry is in deep distress, her hands and fingers are wringing with the intensity of her emotions.

"Take a few deep breaths, Sherry, and let it go," I suggest gently. "That's right."

Then I begin to lead Sherry out of the swamp of her emotions. Since the language of the subconscious is composed of pictures and images, I tap into a visualization technique that will help clear blocked energy and her feelings of failure.

"Sherry, close your eyes and look up at the center of your forehead where insight occurs in your brain and connect with your Higher Power. Silently remember your purpose statement and your symbol as you look upward. Ask your Higher Power to help you by inviting this past discouragement that looks like a dark warehouse to change positively. Watch or sense it as it's changing," I say.

Sherry was able to visualize the warehouse, but she was unable to allow it to change positively. Her hands and fingers told the story of how difficult this was for her to do.

"Take a few deep breaths, Sherry, and it will relax you."

"It's so empty and dark, and I'm scared."

"Stay connected to your Higher Power, Sherry. Stay with it. Keep taking deep breaths . . . you're doing all right."

Not only did Sherry have a hard time getting the empty warehouse to transform, she had even more difficulty verbalizing this, so we used another imaging tool.

I asked Sherry to draw.

At first she didn't want to because she felt she couldn't draw. I reassured her that it wasn't about drawing in an artistic sense. It was about putting down a symbol or stick drawing of whatever you experienced inside of you. Putting emotions down on paper in any visual way helps transform the feelings and get them out.

Sherry did this willingly even though her hands still showed how nervous, anxious, and scared she was. By drawing, Sherry broke through old mental traps that led her to believe and feel she was a failure. The first step of allowing the empty warehouse to transform in her imagination was to pour her feelings of emptiness onto the page.

Sherry showed me her "empty feelings drawing" and explained what she had drawn. It was an empty toothpaste tube, shown from three different angles and an empty glass. This was powerful work for Sherry. She cried for several minutes.

"It's OK to let that past go. It's safe to let it go. It's safe to grow and change," I said. Through this emotional flood, I saw Sherry had released the negative block of emotions that commanded her to see herself as a failure in this situation.

To further help Sherry transform the image of the dark, empty warehouse, I offered her *The Schoolteacher Technique.*

I asked her to write the following sentence 15 times every day in her journal for the next three weeks: *I am sincere and I choose to trust in positive outcomes.* These words concisely convey to Sherry's subconscious her purity of purpose. Writing this continuously for three weeks is the first step to forming a positive habit that will endure. I urged her to practice this for as long as it took to integrate this truth into her cells, eventually causing a complete change in body, mind, and spirit.

At the close of this emotionally moving, clearing session, I told Sherry we would work further on transforming the empty warehouse in future sessions. In conclusion, I encouraged Sherry's progress and gave her a little more understanding about the process in which she was involved.

"Sherry, you did some wonderful work today. I know you've been feeling anxious and discouraged about your perceived progress and you want to go faster, accomplishing your goals according to your expectations and timetable.

"However, please remember that it's important to hold realistic expectations. A part of the process is the rhythm of 'two steps forward, one back.' It's integral to attaining solid equilibrium on each new level you reach.

"It's also natural to feel discouraged at times. Especially when you perceive you might be slipping backward. Any time you make any kind of change, the subconscious and the body knows there's safety of familiarity in the status quo. We often want to stay with old behaviors only because they're familiar—even though those behaviors may be hurtful or self-defeating to us in the long run. This is a part of the paradox of life. Please know that you're doing well and moving forward toward weight balance success," I concluded.

In a matter of six months, Sherry balanced to her perfect weight.

The Schoolteacher Technique

Write I choose to trust in positive outcomes in your journal 15 times each day, at the same time every day, consistently for at least three weeks. Be aware during this period of time how your mind free-associates and connects this phrase with your purpose statement during the day. Look for changes in your life, attitudes, and outlook that reflect results with this exercise.

You can also add a purpose symbol to this statement, or draw a fun doodle image to go with the above statement. Make it silly and light; there's no right or wrong way to do this. Since the language of the subconscious is composed of symbol and image, this technique allows you to talk Soul to Soul (your true divine Self) with instant understanding.

The old habits of the mind are stubborn in their resistance to change. However, committing to practice these techniques and doing them—no matter what—ultimately brings lasting change. In this way, you say "No" to mental programming and old emotions that have held you back in the past. This is the way you choose to be free.

Taking Stock of Your Progress So Far

It's time to review what you've accomplished so far and take stock of your emotional state. Maybe you've been feeling discouraged like Sherry. Maybe your discouragement even verges upon defeat, as hers did. At this point in the journey, it's a common pitfall for many people to minimize the positive steps they've already made. You're not alone if you're feeling this way.

> *So often the mind will skim over the small steps and minimize your progress as a way of denying the truth. The good news is you can choose to view this as a positive road sign. book text, book text book text.*

You can chose to release the denial and allow yourself the opportunity to be involved, motivated, and bold about your progress.

The affirmative statement that works in this case is the same one I gave Sherry in *The Schoolteacher Technique:* "I choose to trust in positive outcomes." It also helps to say, "I am trust" 10, 100, or 1000 times a day. The operative principle here is to say it until it comes true.

This is part of your responsibility and your mission in attaining weight balance success—to deprogram the mind from myths as well as minimizing. You can use both of these affirmation statements with breathing exercises to release deep stress and nurture relaxation as you begin to trust yourself, trust the process, and trust in positive outcomes.

Review List Exercise

    (1) Close your eyes, connect to your Higher Power, and ask, what steps have I taken so far?

    (2) List all the small steps you have taken, such as buying, reading, and practicing the principles outlined in this book. Be sure to count making your purpose statement and every technique, exercise, activity, and visualization you have done in the course of reading this book.

    (3) Read your list aloud to yourself and really understand deep in your heart all you have done in the quest for your goal.

    (4) Again, close your eyes and ask your Higher Power if you missed any steps. Then add any missed steps to your list.

    (5) Ask your Higher Power, "How can I better accept my progress and stay reliable to myself?" Write down the wisdom you receive.

    (6) Ask your Higher Power, "What is my next step?" Jot down what you receive. Take a deep breath and open your eyes when you're ready.

I like to tell the following metaphorical story about the journey to weight balance. In order to traverse the half-mile bridge across my street, I have to take one small step right now to get out the door and start moving toward it. My steps are small. Some people have a larger stride while others have a smaller, slower stride than mine. Yet the way to walk this bridge for everyone is simply by taking one step after another. Maybe it's necessary to take time to rest midway through, and then take more steps. I may stop at the crest of the bridge and want to turn around because I become discouraged. Yet resting refreshes me. Since the remainder of the journey is downhill, it's easier from now on.

You are on a similar journey of weight balance. The *Review List Exercise* is one rest stop. You can choose to stay on course after this rest stop by choosing to be reliable to yourself and your greater purpose.

How to Eliminate Being Stuck

When I think about ways to eliminate being stuck, a thousand possibilities flood my mind. What I've learned from experience is to keep it simple. The following techniques are simple and yet powerful in their ability to free you from being stuck. Choose one or more you'd like to use and practice them.

Brainstorm for Activities

When you're feeling stuck, you can use a brainstorming technique to gather as many ideas and techniques for getting unstuck as you can imagine. The most important thing to do with this technique is to "turn off the censor." *Any* idea has the potential to lead you to the one thing it will take to get unstuck.

To brainstorm, take a large sheet of paper and write "How to Become Unstuck" in the center of the page. Draw a circle around the topic. Next, put any ideas that pop into your mind around it, drawing circles around each idea with a line connecting it to the concept that led to, generated, or helped inspire it in the first place.

When I did this exercise, one of the first ideas I got was to call a supportive person. Reach for the phone and call. Keep your mind free of doubts or thoughts of fear that might have stopped you in the past.

Another idea is to imagine a nearby beautiful place. Get ready and go for a walk where there is beauty. Enjoy the surroundings as best you can. See if anything unusual happens that might relate to your being stuck. Maybe you'll see an animal that's stuck. Maybe you'll decide to help it get unstuck. You could have a number of adventures as you open your eyes and see in a whole new way (maybe the world around you has a symbolic, image-rich message for you about how to get unstuck).

Another idea is to scout around and find a support group. Ask the members if there are other groups they know of and when do they meet? Or turn to the members in your discussion group on this book. Keep pursuing your quest for support.

Another thing to do is draw a stick figure that is stuck using colored markers. Put the title *Being Stuck* into the picture. Ask the figure in the drawing for some insight into the deeper reasons why it is stuck or how to get unstuck. Write down what you receive. Then journal your explanation of your drawing as if you were sharing it with a close, trusted friend or a therapist. Be sure to date your work. Reflect on it for the next week as you look for greater insight and understanding.

As soon as possible, take out your journal and write about being stuck. Write a prayer question, pray for help from your Higher Power, or contemplate on the answer. You can use any of these techniques to help move beyond any feeling of being stuck that you might have.

Before Dealing with Rage and Pain

Gabrielle Roth explores dancing as a release and prayer of emotion in her latest book, *Maps to Ecstasy*. She also has videotapes (*The Wave: Ecstatic Dance for Body and Soul*), CDs and audiocassettes (*The Endless Wave*) that explore using movement as a spiritual practice. She describes releasing feelings in an ancient, profound way through moving meditatively and creatively to music. Free yourself from stuck feelings using her music or select your favorite musical songs to create your own ecstatic dance. The only requirement is being willing to move and let the music direct you.

Dealing with Rage, Anger, and Pain

I once worked with a successful business man (who was consistently stuck in anger and rage) as I did with Sherry in the opening example of this chapter. I asked him to get a visual picture of his anger and rage, leaving himself out of the picture. He saw these emotions embodied in the image of an exploding volcano.

I suggested he continue with the example of the exploding volcano, close his eyes, look upward to the center of his forehead (where insight occurs in the brain), and connect with his Higher Power as he knew it.

Then I said, "Silently ask your Higher Power to help you invite this picture of your past anger and rage to change positively. Watch it change to more closely reflect your purpose statement. Let go of forcing it to change, invite it to change positively, and watch what happens."

He took his time (it works even better when you take more time), and watched. To his amazement, the volcano started to erupt even more.

I asked him to just keep watching the volcano release all of the anger and rage, and tell me what he was experiencing with each change. This is what he described: "At first the volcano exploded more, then it finally stopped, cooled, and began to change geologically into two rolling hills. Then green grass started growing. Finally the sun came out."

"Does that feel complete for you?"

"Yes," he said.

This technique is especially helpful for releasing and moving beyond strong emotions that have set up chronic patterns throughout your lifetime.

Punch a Hologram

The next technique is great for releasing individual episodes of past angers or frustrations. You'll be surprised at the positive results you'll have breaking free once you use this technique. One woman remarked she was able to sleep better than she had in years. Another said she was calmer throughout the week and no longer turned her past anger upon herself in self-punishing behavior. By feeling calmer, she felt motivated to eventually take her next step toward a healthier, balanced diet.

First find a comfortable, safe place where you will be undisturbed for at least 20 minutes. Close your eyes and look upward to the center of your forehead where insight occurs in your brain. Ask your subconscious mind to scan back through the many past angers or frustrations you've experienced in your life. Let the subconscious pick one for you to release now.

Keeping your eyes closed, allow both of your hands to form fists. Make them tight, as if you are clenching the past anger or frustration you want released. Consciously be aware of how tight and tense your fists are. Feel this tightness in your belly and your legs.

In front of you is a hologram. It may be a person you are still angry with, or it may be a symbol of a situation that angers you. Step closer to it. Feel your fists hitting the hologram in your imagination. Hear the slap, smack, or pop sounds. Each time you hit this hologram, release more of your past angers or frustrations. Keep on doing this until you feel you've released all of it. You may yell silently in your imagination to release even more past anger. It is important to take all the time you need. The more time you take to do this, the better.

When you feel the exercise is complete, take a deep cleansing breath. Relax your hands and body. The image of the hologram will disappear and once again, you are in your safe, quiet place.

Say aloud, "I choose to trust in positive outcomes." Connect again with your Higher Power and ask for help in reflecting on what you've learned. After you do this, write the answers to the following questions in your journal:

(1) What did I learn?
(2) What is different now from my releasing all this anger and frustration?

Feel, Question, Change Technique

For this exercise, let's explore a specific emotion, such as guilt. Suppose you feel guilty. Ask yourself, what does guilt look like? Let the first picture of what guilt looks like pop into your mind. Guilt probably wouldn't look like a dozen red roses. Maybe it looks more like rust eating a fairly new car.

Close your eyes and look upward to the insight area between your eyes. Ask your Higher Power to help you to allow this past guilty feeling to change in an uplifting way. Maybe you start to become part of changing the situation by sanding away the rust and preparing the car for a new paint job in your imagination. After you finish sanding, maybe you spray on a few coats of paint in your favorite color, until the car looks brand-new. Take your time; keep asking for more change, keep watching and imagining. You'll know when it's complete. When it is finished, thank your Higher Power for helping you be free of this past guilt.

Now picture or sense a door in front of you. Notice the color and any other details, like the knob, how it is made, or its finish. As you open the door and walk through it, know that you are stepping into a new level of awareness and freedom, furthering you on your journey to weight balance success.

The Five Senses Technique

What the *Five Senses Technique* does is elevate the thought of being stuck to a higher level of the brain in order to clear it. To do this, you'll be using all five senses as passkeys to create an image or symbol that speaks to the subconscious while sweeping it clean.

Let's say you are feeling stuck with the negative thought *Nothing is ever going to change.* Close you eyes and look upward to connect to your Higher Power. Ask yourself, what color is this feeling of being stuck, as you allow the first thing you think of to pop into your mind. Now think to yourself, where do I keep this feeling in my body?

Next, let an image connected to this feeling just pop into your mind (even if it doesn't make sense). Now this stuck feeling that's a certain color which you keep in a certain place in your body that's connected to an image, how big does it feel? Does it feel as big as this room? Define how big this feeling is in relation to you.

Now let a sound pop into your mind. Then think of a smell and or a taste.

Express this feeling of being stuck with a hand movement of some kind. If you believe "I don't know how," just imagine you *do* know how and let your hands express the movement. Do it now.

Finally, ask your Higher Power to give you a tool to get rid of this feeling of being stuck and all the negative thoughts and images that tag along with it. Conceive of using the tool to get rid of every single piece of this feeling, the negative thoughts, and the images, down to the essence of your cells.

If you need to use your imagination or your creativity to make yourself huge or your tool gigantic, then do so—whatever works. Take your time and make sure every atom of the feeling is gone.

Take a deep cleansing breath. See yourself and know you are accomplishing your purpose. Think about your purpose symbol and see yourself taking one more step toward your goal.

In summary, any one of these techniques will help free you from being stuck in any negative emotion. Each technique is simple but powerful in its results. You'll alter the dynamic and change the cycle after you do one of these techniques. Saying aloud "I choose to trust in positive outcomes" afterward will help bring a wind of change into your life.

Now remember a time in your life when you felt free. Tap into that feeling and try one of the techniques mentioned previously right now. Try it and feel free.

If You're Doubtful at Times, Here's What to Do

This doubt-busting technique is relatively simple. Just choose one practical, down-to-earth thing to do and do it with love, while asking inwardly to be open to a new spiritual awareness or answer. It's often in the humblest of places that we find answers. It's just a matter of having the humility to bend down and look for them.

This story about a phone man illustrates this "do it with love" attitude. It occurred about two weeks after I began using a new phrase (*I am love*) with "The Schoolteacher Technique." I was thinking of this phrase as I directed the phone repair man to check out the phone jack in the bedroom.

Although he was relatively young (in his mid-thirties, dressed in a T-shirt and jeans), he had already developed a large potbelly. When he saw the stairs, he said, "I wouldn't want to climb these very often."

The phone man resented the stairs and the concept of any extra physical effort. His resentments stopped him from getting into better physical shape and moving forward in consciousness. Resentments, like doubts, can hold us back. To me, the stairs represented an opportunity to give myself more health through physical effort.

I said, "I love them. They help me keep in shape. I like to run up and down them. My heart loves the aerobic action, too."

Putting love into all you do will help you progress physically, emotionally, mentally, and spiritually. Even stairs can be seen as a blessing of health when accepted with eyes of loving awareness.

You Always Have a Choice in How You Respond

When you're feeling hopelessness, helpless, powerless, and don't know consciously how to access your power and leave these feelings behind, it's often easy to act in controlling ways toward yourself and toward others. In the following example, Jenny discovers that she has a choice in how she responds.

Once during a business meeting, a co-worker asked Jenny to pick up a client at the airport. Inwardly Jenny felt this was a hassle, beneath her job description, and she just didn't want to do it. Jenny was furious at her friend for asking but found she couldn't say no, so she agreed to meet the plane. Then Jenny felt hurt, trapped, and hostile. She began to pout by looking down at her notebook and stopped interacting at the meeting.

Situations such as this had happened many times in the past. Usually Jenny would go home and eat, stuffing her anger. However this time, Jenny's boss confronted her.

"You're controlling everyone in this room," she said. "You haven't said a word, but you've had everyone's attention for the last fifteen minutes. You know it too—you're smiling."

Shocked and ashamed, Jenny knew it was true, for she felt like laughing even as she was being confronted about her angry, controlling behavior.

Her boss continued, "If you make the choice to use that energy in a positive, purposeful way, you'd be a powerful being who could accomplish anything."

Jenny was hit with the truth. Powerful? Angry and controlling? Accomplish anything? She knew she felt like an ashamed little girl and began to wonder about the dynamics of the dichotomy that triggered her urge to laugh.

This was turning point for Jenny. She gradually became more aware of her behavior and its effect on others, even when she felt helpless and didn't fully know what she was doing. Deep inside, Jenny knew she was a powerful spiritual being. But she also knew she had bought too heavily in to the societal belief that it was more acceptable to be helpless.

That day Jenny learned what it feels like to be on the dark side of control, allowing herself to be controlled and the flip side of manipulating and controlling others. When Jenny negated her feelings by agreeing to do what she did not want to do, she denied her own truth and undermined her true self.

Jenny might have handled the situation differently. She could have asked for support and help from others at the meeting—but she didn't. It was easier for Jenny to act out of past habits and patterns. Well after the event, Jenny realized she had a choice in how she could respond. The simple truth is this: Jenny could have responded by just saying, "No."

Learning to Say No and Feel Good about It

The following story is about using creativity to learn ways to say "No" to what you don't want in your life so that there's more room for you to say "Yes" to what you do want.

A woman named Kathryn wrote in her new journal, "I'd like to dedicate this journal to creating spiritual writing exercises to bring more freedom into my life."

Inwardly Kathryn knew what was keeping her from experiencing the level of freedom she wanted, since she had struggled with guilt most of her life. This guilt connected to many weed-like beliefs and behaviors, such as (1) Kathryn believed she wasn't good enough; (2) she thought everything that went wrong was her fault; (3) she felt compelled to please others; (4) she felt responsible for fixing everyone's problems; and (5) she couldn't say no to other people's requests for her time and energy. Underlying these beliefs, Kathryn discovered she held unrealistic expectations of herself, namely that she needed to be perfect and liked by everyone. Both of these expectations stemmed from a false sense of vanity rooted in low self-esteem.

Kathryn's first step to healing her faulty belief system was learning to say no to the many demands on her resources. She began this process by writing NO in eight-inch high, black letters across her front door to remind her to say it whenever she could. Whenever Kathryn *did* say no however, she noticed a high degree of anxiety and guilt would result.

Kathryn realized her underlying guilt was blocking her progress toward developing the ability to say no. She knew the only way she could feel good about herself was to go deeper in her quest, simultaneously confronting and dealing with both major issues (learning to say no *and* absolving her guilt). Here's how she did it.

Kathryn wrote the words "LET IT GO" on several yellow index cards and placed them at strategic points around house. Whenever she saw these cards, it reminded her subconscious to let go of guilty feelings. Also, whenever she started to feel guilty, she would command herself in loud, forcible words to "LET IT GO!" She practiced saying this throughout the day.

She not only found that the command words helped her release feelings of guilt and perfectionism, today she only has to hear these words and she instantly relaxes. These command words will work for you in a similar manner once you've mastered this technique.

Kathryn also practiced many different ways of saying "No" using the *Assertiveness Scripts* that follow (see sidebar on page 81) until it became comfortable for her to segue them into casual conversation. All of this happened gradually in a natural cycle of change. Kathryn took the process of change little by little, step-by-step, all the while receiving just what she could handle, at the pace she could handle.

Kathryn found when she mastered the ability to say no, she was finally free of the guilt that had once plagued her. And when most of her energy wasn't tied up emotionally with faulty beliefs, her eating habits began to improve too.

Kathryn used the following journal technique to stay on target in mastering ways to say "No" in disagreements and discussions.

Targeting the Bull's-Eye Technique

First she drew a picture of a bull's-eye target in her journal. She wrote the word NO in bold letters directly in the center. Then she drew long arrows, reaching from the edge of the page to the center of the target. Then Kathryn drifted into a light contemplation and thought about the last opportunity she'd had to say no and failed (a weekly phone call from her mother complaining about other members of the family). In her mind, she replayed the conversation from start to finish.

Instead of clenching her jaw and allowing the situation to frustrate her, Kathryn focused on what she wanted to change about the conversation—namely her responses. Again, she used the *Assertiveness Scripts* to help prompt her. Each time Kathryn came up with a good counter-response to her mother's complaining, she wrote it down in her journal along the shaft of one of the arrows that pointed to the bull's-eye NO. She knew as she did this exercise, she was getting closer to her goal of being able to say "No" in actual conversation. Kathryn used this exercise, drawing a new bull's-eye target for each life situation she encountered where she wanted more clarity on how she could have handled it better by saying "No."

Assertiveness Scripts

> *(1) Disagree* with a straightforward statement ("I don't agree with your understanding of . . .")
>
> *(2) Confront* by denying the statement is relevant to the conversation ("That's not the point.")
>
> *(3) Reword* negative labels by framing it in positive words ("I am not being childish; I'm stating my view.")
>
> *(4) Repeat* your main point until it is heard without anger
>
> *(5) Ask Questions* if you're not comfortable with a point, or ask for clarification ("How do you see me as childish?")
>
> *(6) State Feelings* by using "I" statements that reflect your opinion about the situation ("I really feel this is important!")
>
> *(7) Be Short and Quick* by just saying "NO" directly

You may look at these scripts and think to yourself, "That's all well and good, but it won't work in my situation because (fill in your specific reason why it won't work here)."

After mentally explaining your doubts to yourself, stop for a moment and ask, "Do I feel better or worse after explaining why it won't work for me?" In other words, do you feel more motivated toward your goal after explaining why it won't work, or do you feel let-down and a loss of energy? What did you discover? If you skimmed over these questions, didn't weigh the answers for yourself, or didn't do the targeting exercise, go back, read them again, and do the exercise with a willingness to measure your inner energetic results. You might learn something new about yourself.

Using an assertive script is the first step. You'll find when you learn to say "No" to the things you no longer want in your life, it makes much more room for you to say "Yes" to the things you do want.

A Simple Technique of Choice

(1) Upon rising go to the mirror, look into your eyes and say with determination, "I have a choice."

(2) Look in your right eye first and say, "I have a choice" three times.

(3) Next look into your left eye and say "I have a choice" three times.

(4) Then look at your whole face and say, "I have a choice" three times.

(5) Do this morning, noon, and before bedtime. Each time say it with passion. Act "as-if" your attitude toward being open, prepared, and purposeful in your quest toward weight balance success is manifesting more every minute. You will get what you expect.

(6) Stay open during the day and be aware of how your attitude changes. Be willing to honor yourself, your style, and your intuition. Be ready to be flexible to unforeseen circumstances as reality shifts in unexpected ways to ultimately accommodate your goals.

Being Willing to Do Whatever Is Needed

What comes next is learning to say "No" to negative feelings and behaviors *while feeling good within yourself and about yourself.* Ask yourself, "Am I willing? Am I willing to do whatever is needed to reach my goal, staying firm and on purpose?" With as much emotion as you can imagine or conceive of, say or silently think this affirmation: "I am willing to do whatever is needed to reach my goal and support my purpose with my actions." Remember your subconscious is listening, so give it your sincere best.

How to "Feel Good"

If you've never felt really positive about who you are during your whole life, it's a tall order to fill when you first start to want to feel good. Try right now to recall some memories of when you felt good. Maybe you remember feeling good when you ate ice cream with Dad. Or maybe you felt good from a lover's touch or from a hot bath. Maybe you felt good after reaching a goal that's taken months or years to accomplish. Maybe engaging in your favorite hobby or competing in a sport makes you feel good.

Ask yourself the following questions: "What feels good to me? What qualities would be part of an experience of feeling good?" One woman started this exercise by listing the things she knew did *not* make her feel good—things she no longer wanted in her life. Her list looked like the following:

"What I Do *Not* Want" List

> (1) No morbid thoughts about my body
> (2) No more exhaustion
> (3) No more stuffing myself until I sleep
> (4) No more thoughts of hating myself or my mate
> (5) No more abusing my body with purging or restricting
> (6) No more stuffing my anger and not talking about it
> (7) No more second-guessing or doubting myself in my thoughts or feelings
> (8) No more isolating myself due to fear or grief
> (9) No more reacting to guilt arising from habit, based on faulty beliefs—not true reality

These points of what she did not want in her life anymore were prompted by the *43 Symptoms to Heed* in Chapter 2. By practicing the following exercise, you can turn your "don't wants" into affirmative keys that unlock knowing what you *do* want in your life.

"What I *Do* Want" List

> (1) "No more morbid thoughts about my body" *transforms into* "I choose to accept my body. I choose to feel complete and at peace inside my body."
> (2) "No more exhaustion" *transforms into* "I choose to feel relaxed in my body. I choose to feel balanced in all my activities."
> (3) "No more stuffing myself until I sleep" *transforms into* "I choose actions to make me feel better about myself."

(4) "No more thoughts of hating myself or my mate" *transforms into* "I choose to be gentle and loving with myself and others."

(5) "No more abusing my body with purging or restricting" *transforms into* "I choose to be kinder to myself. I can discover ways to be my own best friend more every day."

(6) "No more stuffing my anger and not talking about it" *transforms into* "I choose to be willing to learn the steps to safely change and grow in understanding my anger."

(7) "No more doubting (second-guessing) my thoughts or feelings" *transforms into* "I am on my way to letting go of doubting myself."

(8) "No more isolating myself due to fear or grief" *transforms into* "I choose to be willing to create a ladder that begins to put me into healthy activities and around supportive people who nurture the new me."

(9) "No more reacting to guilt arising from habit, based on faulty beliefs—not true reality" *transforms into* "I choose to catch my reactions to my doubts and my guilt before I act upon them. I choose to actively seek new, life-enhancing behaviors."

These affirmations change what you don't want into what you do want. Take a deep breath. As you let your breath out, silently tell yourself to relax. Take another deep breath and slowly breath the air out, all the while saying to yourself, "Relax." Really *mean it* as you tell your shoulders to relax. Then tell your jaw to relax and feel it. Say, "I give myself permission to relax. It is safe to relax and grow."

Any one of these transformed statements can be made into a reality and brought more quickly into your life by using it in *The Schoolteacher Technique*. This is one way to say *yes* to bring good things into your life.

Resisting the Urge to Quit

A woman named Joyce tried the previous exercise. However, after doing the "don't want list," she became overwhelmed, overwrought, and felt just plain inadequate.

In the past, whenever Joyce felt overwhelmed, overwrought, or inadequate, she would drop whatever was overwhelming her, go fix herself a big plate of pasta, pizza, or bagels, (and a chocolate bar or two), and eat it. After she'd finished eating, the feeling of being overwhelmed would completely disappear. Joyce didn't realize this escape mechanism of "turning on" to food was her way to magically make the negative feelings go away.

Joyce never took the time to transform the statements into positive affirmations by completing the "do want list" part of the exercise. Her reaction at this point was to just quit: quit doing the affirmation exercises and quit striving for weight balance.

When old feelings of being overwhelmed, overwrought, inadequate, and guilt kick in, old behavioral coping mechanisms and habits automatically take over, unless you choose to act in a take-charge kind of way to change that right now.

Start your own list. Change all the reasons why you can't do it and want to quit into transformational statements of affirmation, such as, "I am choosing to be open, prepared, and purposeful in my quest for weight balance success." Choose to be open and on target with your actions—keep reading! You can do it by first taking a series of deep belly breaths. Belly breaths help center and relax you.

Like a book, when we stay open, we have the opportunity to gain more tools, knowledge, and wisdom. If we're closed, there is no way to gain these gifts of greater understanding from the universe or our Higher Power. This is a most important key. Stay open, keep this book open, and keep reading!

Practical Tools to Find More Answers

Recently, Sherry often felt stuck and frustrated. She was trying hard to choose different actions so that she didn't return to escaping her emotions by eating, or distracting herself in endless pursuits of pleasure as she had done in the past.

I found the biggest clue as to why Sherry was stuck and frustrated is in her word "trying." Trying is not doing; it is simply attempting, yet failing once again. When someone is trying, they're really not ready to take action toward change. There's a subtle shift between trying and doing, but it makes all the difference in the world between staying stuck and attaining your dreams.

This is what it takes to be free of the old mental patterns that enslave us without our conscious awareness. It is mysterious because it remains unknown, hidden in the subconscious of the person experiencing enslaving thought patterns. So Sherry was caught once again in the self-defeating, negative inner self-talk of her unconscious.

In the following story, Sherry manifests a breakthrough contemplation experience, reflecting her willingness to change. It also shows the ever-present support and assistance of her Higher Power, which is just waiting for a sign from Sherry that she's ready and willing to move into a state of transformation.

Sherry wrote to me about some experiential work she was doing. One morning she had a vision during contemplation. She wrote, "I was in a chrysalis and a couple of helpers in my life were there to support me. I was aware of them energetically around the chrysalis, cheering me on. However, even though I pushed my head backward against the encasing energy, the chrysalis was too solid for me to break through."

Because Sherry journals, practices the techniques in this book, and relies on her Higher Power for daily guidance, she spontaneously knew she could ask for help and get it at this critical time. "Please, I need help," she wrote in her journal. Because she surrendered enough to ask for help, the message broke through to her subconscious, illuminating the deeper meaning of the vision in her mind.

What Sherry didn't realize at the time was she was observing the situation as she was taking action. It was only when she reviewed her journal account of the experience later that she stumbled on the insight that the helpers surrounding her were connected to her Higher Power.

The symbol of the chrysalis showed not only how trapped she was in hostility, but that the process of transformation was imminent. I explained how she could work with the chrysalis image in her imagination to stop "trying" to free herself from the old mental thought patterns and start actually doing it. Here's the next step of this creative process that you can do, too.

The Butterfly Technique: **An Imaginative Exercise for Empowering the Next Step**

1. *Before going to sleep, record in your journal that you want to invite the state of being in a chrysalis to change positively.*
2. *Imagine putting this request into the hands of your Higher Power.*
3. *Now close your eyes and imagine yourself in a warm, relaxed, comfortable state encased inside a chrysalis.*
4. *Visualize your Higher Power and Its helpers surrounding the chrysalis. Each of them has a tube of chrysalis-dissolving fluid.*
5. *Observe carefully how each helper squeezes some fluid on the tip of the chrysalis and rubs it in. See the chrysalis-dissolving fluid begin to dissolve the material encasing you in everyday problems and stuck behavioral responses this lifetime. Your Higher Power and Its helpers are gently and thoroughly rubbing the dissolving fluid on the surface of the chrysalis. Remember, you are the spiritual butterfly within the chrysalis.*

Now shift your attention from watching what is happening outside the chrysalis to being inside the chrysalis. Feel the dissolving fluid rubbed into the area surrounding your head. Feel the encasement of a lifetime begin to dissolve. Soon your head is free. Your Higher Power and Its helpers cheer you, "Hey, you in there, come on out."

They watch as you break free of the human emotions and behaviors that have trapped you in the past. When this happens, the sun seems to come from behind a cloud and shines brilliantly upon you, melting the remainder of the chrysalis. You hear the sounds of nature (use your imagination to manifest this). Do this exercise each night for about a month. You'll experience progress and more freedom in your life.

Allow Change

Practice *The Butterfly Technique* to help free yourself from hardened attitudes and old states of consciousness connected to diet myths, as well as empower your next step toward a new consciousness—one which embraces weight balance success. Be patient with yourself and keep in mind that the process of transformation is often a gradual one (like the butterfly breaking free of the chrysalis).

To expedite change, say the following words five times a day: "I allow these changes into my life." Saying these words is a way to allow yourself to experience and learn new things. It is a way you can be supportive of yourself as you take the time to become skilled at something new.

To review:

1. Commit to singing your love song to yourself each day at the same time daily.

2. Practice *The Schoolteacher Technique* by writing "I choose to trust in positive outcomes" or another affirmative statement that furthers you toward your goal, contributes to clearing blocks, or frees you from feeling stuck. Write the positive affirmation at least 15 times daily.

3. List all the positive, small steps you have taken toward your goal. Write down everything you can remember. Ask your Higher Power, "How can I better accept my progress and stay reliable to myself?" Write down what you receive. Ask your Higher Power, "What is my next step?" Jot down what you receive.

4. Brainstorm possible ways to move beyond being stuck. Experiment with one or more of the imaginative techniques and visualizations given in the brainstorming section of this chapter.

5. Do one practical, down-to-earth thing each day with love, while asking inwardly to be open to a new spiritual awareness or answer.

6. Journal about the situations or events in your life which you have a choice about how you respond. If appropriate, practice *The Bull's-Eye Target Technique* with the *Assertiveness Scripts* to foster the ability to say no to those things you no longer want in your life. Briefly record your experiences with this in your journal.

7. Practice *The Butterfly Technique* to get unstuck and empower your next step. While keeping in mind that transformation is a gradual process (like the butterfly), say the following words five times a day: "I allow these changes in my life." Practice patience with yourself on your journey to weight balance success.

Chapter 7 explores a dozen ways to interpret your dreams and rediscover your true self. It also offers techniques for combining creativity and imagination to make your dreams come true, as well as sharing ways to receive the love you need while maintaining your success.

Part 2
Learning To Be Free

Chapter 7
Dreams, Creativity and Imagination

Getting Clear on How You Want To Be

Where do you start? Just the thought of dreaming how you want to be can conjure up images of living your wildest dreams. So let the wildest dreams come out! A woman named Katie said, "I'd like to be slim and healthy, have clear skin, a boyfriend, and tons of fun experiences." Try the following fun, imaginative, writing exercise and see how far it takes you in establishing a vision of your future—the first step to making your dreams come true.

My Wildest Dreams Come True Writing Exercise

1. My wildest dream is to be _____.
2. My wildest dream is to be _____.
3. My wildest dream is to be _____.
4. In my wildest dream, I have _____.
5. In my wildest dream, I have _____.
6. In my wildest dream, I have _____.
7. In my wildest dream, I look like _____.
8. In my wildest dream, I feel like _____.
9. In my wildest dream, I think _____.
10. In my wildest dream, I know _____.

You can make this a continuing writing exercise by adding to it in your journal for as long as you like. In fact, this is an excellent tool for uplifting your thoughts and focusing your attitudes and actions toward shaping your future in an ongoing daily vision quest. Regular attention on dreaming, believing, and infusing the future of your life with love will help bring a new tomorrow into reality sooner.

The following story illustrates how faith and imagination combined with creativity and action helped Katie bring her dreams of the future one step closer as she changed her life.

Katie came from a home where her mother constantly criticized her. Katie's mom would say, "You aren't like me. You eat too much and you're stupid. Why can't you do things right? You're no better than white trash people; you don't belong here with me." Katie's mom pushed her away and threw Katie into her room. She yelled at her and beat her, telling her she was a bad girl. Katie tried to be good and do all her chores, but she was always hungry because her mother gave her so little to eat.

One day Katie went into the woods, sat down, and began to cry. She cried so hard it seemed that she would never stop. The more she cried, the more hopeless and distressed she felt.

This cycle continued all through her adolescent years until her mother became ill and needed Katie to take care of her. Katie did the best she could. She washed the clothes, the dishes, and cleaned the house. She even tried to prepare the food. However, she didn't know how to since her mother had fed her so poorly and she never learned.

One night Katie had a dream. In the dream she was outside sitting in the woods, crying because she felt so miserable about her life. She looked up once and found a woman standing beside her who asked, "Why are you crying?"

Katie answered, "Nothing I do seems good enough. My mother is sick and I can't even take care of her properly. All I want to do is stuff myself with any food I can find and when I can't stop, I feel awful. I hate that I'm so fat. If only I could do something right, be thin, have beautiful skin and a boyfriend like the other girls at school."

The woman said, "Katie, dry your eyes and I will tell you how to reverse your feelings of deprivation. Say to your Higher Power, "I am choosing to be fulfilled. I am choosing to be complete within myself." Write these statements fifteen times a day for three weeks. Watch your life for changes and be grateful as the changes come, knowing they'll bring the highest good into your life."

The woman assured Katie that her life would change for the better if she did this. She also encouraged Katie to check out some books from the library on improving her food choices and her health. Then the woman vanished.

Katie thought, "I must try this at once. I'm so tired of being sad." She looked up through the trees to the blue sky and with all her heart she called out, "Higher Power I choose to be fulfilled; I choose to be complete within myself." Scarcely had she uttered the words when a purring cat appeared beside her, rubbing up against her leg. Katie picked up the cat. So much love flowed from this cat to Katie in her dream that Katie started feeling wonderful. She sat and petted the cat for a long time, feeling more love and contentment as she did.

The dream affected Katie profoundly. From this dream, she knew she could always connect with the love inside her, as symbolized in her dream by the cat. When she woke up the next morning however, her mother was still sick in bed.

Katie did the housework and began to change how she ate. She started to write the statement the wise woman had given her in the dream in her journal fifteen times every day before she went to bed. In time, Katie's weight balanced and her skin cleared up—mainly because she chose to align her actions with a changed attitude by including more wholesome foods in her life.

One night Katie dreamed she and the cat were walking through the woods when a handsome young man drove up in his Jeep. The man stopped and asked Katie to show him the way to the north road. "Sure," Katie said, agreeing to ride along with him. As they drove along Katie smiled and chatted comfortably with him. She was having a great time. She sensed he really liked her. The dream was so vivid and real. When Katie awoke, she said, "Wow, what an experience." She knew she had been dreaming one of her possible futures, a future filled with love.

What you hold in your consciousness, even on the subtlest, subconscious level of your dreams, gives you the ability to write your own future. Understanding this to the finite cells of your being enables you to make your dreams come true. All it requires is the skill to focus and take one purposeful step after another in the direction you want to go. Everything you need to make your wildest dreams come true is *already inside you.*

Dream Time

Do you remember your dreams? Do you believe dreams hold powerful messages? Have your dreams come true? Have you dreamed of the past or the future? How can dreams help you shape your body/your life? What techniques can you use to better remember your dreams?

Dreaming is not just rest-and-unwind downtime.

> *Dreams can access higher levels of wisdom that directly benefit all aspects of your daily life. These higher levels also allow you to explore the world from a much wider perspective.*

This chapter highlights techniques you can use to expand your dream time for greater experiences, and gives tools you can use to better interpret and understand those experiences, among other things.

What follows is only a small part of the totality of dream knowledge. If you practice the simple techniques described here, you will learn ways to use them for your growth and purpose. Have fun using these techniques and greater peace of mind will follow.

Higher Power Technique

 1. *Say to your Higher Power, "I am choosing to be fulfilled. I am choosing to be complete within myself."*
 2. *Write this same statement fifteen times a day for three weeks.*
 3. *Be willing to receive the changes in whatever form they come. Record the changes in your journal.*
 4. *After three months, review what you have recorded by looking at it from a spiritual perspective.*

Accessing Higher Insight and Understanding the Messages of Dreams

At a spiritual level, we can access answers to anything we want to know. Here is a technique you can use before you go to sleep to help you access higher insight through your dreams.

Before going to bed, relax and decide upon awakening that you will know the answer to whatever you specifically want to know. Put this in the form of a request addressed to your Higher Power, such as "Higher Power, if it's for the greater good, please show me the reason why (fill in your specific request here)."

Maybe you'll ask your Higher Power for the next step on your journey. Maybe you'll ask your Higher Power to show you insights about what you're doing. Maybe you'll ask to understand the reason why you resent the choices you've made in your life. Or you might ask to be shown how to let go of self-hatred, which is the truth hiding beneath the attitudes of regret, annoyance, frustration, or guilt.

These clever disguises for self-hatred are dangerous in that they subliminally undermine your efforts to birth the life you need. They often lead you to act out or escape into old destructive patterns, such as eating, spending, drinking, or looking for love through sex.

By asking for answers in your dreams and expecting to know the answers when you awaken, you can create your new self and birth the life you need with the love that's already inside of you. The following story shows how I came face-to-face with my self-hate and found the means to defeat it by using this simple technique.

Feeling of hate and self-destruction accompanied me for some time, sapping my energy and leaving me with a lingering depression. One day I wrote in my journal, "All I see around me is useless structures everywhere, ways I minimize my years of hard work. I am obsessed with asking myself, 'Is it worth it?' and it takes all my energy to muster up the strength to yell, 'Yes, it is!' I have to break free of this morass and reverse the negative mind set."

That night I wrote, "What I have built is good overall, only it needs to be polished and restructured. I clear these past negative thoughts and surrender them to my Higher Power."

Then I invited myself to be peaceful and take a moment to appreciate myself and all that I had accomplished. Before I went to sleep, I relaxed and decided that when I woke up I would have the answer to peace and self-appreciation. I went to sleep with my dream journal near my bed, knowing that at the moment of my awakening direct truth would be in my conscious awareness.

When I awoke, the dream I'd been dreaming was in the forefront of my mind. A feeling of peace and acceptance pervaded my being and I knew the dream I'd been having held the answer to the question I'd brought up the previous night. Immediately I began to take notes on my dream in my journal.

I dreamed I was descending an escalator with a friend whom I love and admire with all my heart. Carol was behind me, criticizing the one man in the world whom I most admire and love more than anything or anyone else. Surprisingly, I wanted to know more about my friend's negative insights about this much admired man's ego defects as she saw them.

Inwardly I was shocked. It disturbed me deeply to feel that a part of me expressed these negative attitudes in the dream. I realized from this dream experience what vanity feels like. I recognized gossip and criticism as the most blatant forms of vanity. I also realized that they always reflect back destructively upon the sender.

Then I got another shock and tears began to pour down my face. *This is what I am doing to myself.* The man I love and admire most in the dream symbolized what I love and admire most in myself (my spiritual side). I realized I destroy myself daily through self-hate and by demeaning what I have accomplished in life. And every time I criticize someone I love, I do the same to myself spiritually. I really got the truth of the situation in that moment. I decided then and there to take action and let go of criticizing myself, as well as others. I knew I needed to forgive myself for what I had unconsciously done. I did so in writing at the end of chronicling the dream. Then I thanked my Higher Power in writing for giving me the truth through this dream experience.

In the past I had read about this idea of loving yourself more, *but I needed to have the experience* to know the truth about really loving myself. The dream state can be an invaluable tool for giving us the experiences we need to move on and feel good about ourselves, if only we have the ears to listen. We each have our own dream symbols with special meanings for us. The following example illustrates this.

Releasing Destructive Patterns by Diagramming Dreams

The following night I relaxed and decided I'd have the answer to resolving the depression that had arisen from feeding these useless, unproductive attitudes when I awoke.

The next morning I wrote about a series of dreams I had. First I wrote them out longhand, synopsis-style. Then I set up a four-column chart to analyze them. Here's what I wrote:

I dreamed I was a young mother at a dark party. I felt trapped in a hot tub with a gang of teenage boys. One killed me by slicing a knife across my throat. I flew out of my body and over their heads, circling them as I scared them back.

In the next dream scene I was looking through my mother's jewelry box. I was searching for a specific pearl bracelet I wanted my daughter to wear in her wedding. I found many pearls, but persisted until I found the right pearl bracelet.

In the third scene of the dream, I pulled up a plant to bring home. Some women at my house discounted my treasured plant. I took it into another room and saw its stem turn bright purple like pokeweed. The young leaves resembled baby spinach leaves. I knew the pokeweed plant is poisonous; only the new leaves or root tubers can be eaten safely.

After I wrote down the dreams, I divided the next page into four columns. I designated the first column for dream symbols, the second column for free-associating the meaning of the symbols, the third column for questions that arose from the perceived meanings, and the fourth column for answers to the questions. During the process of filling in the diagram, I found the answer to understanding and resolving my depression.

First, I listed each dream symbol in the left column, allowing plenty of room between them. In the second column, I wrote the very first thing I associated with each symbol—even if it didn't make sense. Next I let a question evolve from the free-associated meanings. Lastly, I turned to my Higher Power in contemplation for answers to the questions. The combined answers to the questions gave me a few sentences that succinctly answered my original question of how to resolve the depression I'd fostered from feeding useless attitudes. My example follows. You can try this technique at home with your dreams, too.

Dream Symbol	Meaning	Question	Answer
MOTHER	Mothering Overprotective	What part of me mothers? What do I care for most in myself?	My discipline My spiritual journey
HOT TUB	Contained heat	What hot feeling do I safely contain?	Self-hate
KNIFE KILLED	Stabbing, cutting in a final violent ending	What do I want to eliminate or cut out of my life? What will I do anything to end?	My hate
THROAT	Trust	How is trust killed?	Hate kills the trust I put in my creative spirit
FLEW	To freely rise above	What do I rise above and become free of?	I want to rise above and let go of self-hate
BRACELET	Commitment	What commitment do I make?	To continue with my spiritual growth
PEARL	Irritant transformed into radiant beauty	What irritation can be transformed into beauty?	Resentments
DAUGHTER	Feminine youth	What part of me is youthful and feminine?	My renewed joy of life
WEDDING	To publicly commit to be wed or united	What do I want to be drawn more closely to through a public committment?	My spiritual growth
TREASURED PLANT	Valued growth	What values grow naturally within?	Understanding and spiritual expansion
POKEWEED	Poisonous with age	What grows more poisonous and destructive with maturity?	Unresolved resentments

Here's the message I received from the analysis: I must use self-discipline to protect my growth and progress on my spiritual journey. Self-hatred or any kind of hate I allow myself to feel kills trust and my creative spirit. I can rise above and let go of hate and resentment in order to continue to grow on my spiritual journey. Resentment can be transformed into a renewed joy of life with understanding. Long-standing resentments can be recognized, resolved, and risen above with spiritual expansion as another step in my spiritual growth.

Journal Pages to Prompt Dream Wisdom and Help You Find Change

Date:

Question:

Purpose:

Dream(s) or Waking Dreams Synopsis:

Diagram (on the back of the page)

Insight:

Action taken:

The analogy of the pearl bracelet is also my commitment to purity in my spiritual goals. I try to continually turn life's irritations into pearls of wisdom, love and mercy towards all life—like oysters turn specks of sand into beauty. By resolving resentments with truth and kindness when it's necessary, I can be like that pure pearl, too.

I've given my daughter the symbolism of pearls so that she will understand the process of turning life's troubles and sorrows into precious gems of strength. The process of writing down, analyzing, and interpreting your dreams is one way to develop this strength.

Persistence in Journaling

When you start journaling your dreams, you may find that your writing voice is undeveloped, even awkward, like a small child's—mine was too when I began journaling dreams in the 1980s. Your first dream writings may make little sense to you at first. I admit this was true for me, too.

However when you persevere in recording and analyzing your dreams, they will tell you exactly what you need to know to live a freer, happier, more fulfilled life. Persist in writing and analyzing your dream wisdom so blessings may continue to come into your life, turning your dreams of the future into realities.

The Power of Taking Just One More Step

Sometimes the art of taking just one more step can radically change the course of your life for the better forever. It can be as simple as getting a good night's rest so you can begin with a new outlook the next day or as dramatic and life-changing as the following dream and its accompanying life story illustrates.

About sixteen years ago, I dreamed I survived an enormous hurricane and found myself struggling with the aftermath. Rubble surrounded me and a strange smell hung in the air. I climbed over beams and under roofs. I fell and scratched my knees and legs, and even twisted an ankle. Yet I knew I needed and wanted to keep moving forward. I knew I wanted to survive.

The path soon became steep. I leaned forward and willed my legs to keep walking. Yet I wondered about the prospect of going back. "Why am I doing this?" I asked myself. "This is crazy. I could go back." Yet I felt compelled to keep moving forward, taking just one more step, and then another, through the rubble.

I felt frustrated and hopeless. I was so tired I could barely see where I was going. I almost turned back. Finally the path opened into a valley nestled between two foothills. I realized I had entered a bowl-shaped crater carved out by the forceful hurricane winds.

The devastation from the hurricane lay strewn around me. I started looking for things I could use to survive. I found a leather tool belt—the kind carpenters wear—and buckled it around my hips. I scanned the surrounding countryside and saw scattered tools and supplies: an ax, a hammer, a pocket utility knife, a plastic jug of water, and some rope.

I gathered the tools and hung them in the leather holders and pockets of the tool belt. Each time I put one into my belt, I felt the power of its possibilities. The events made sense on a profound level. I stood tall with the leather belt supported on my hips, feeling completely safe. I knew I was entering another stage of my journey and felt excited about getting started.

I opened up to the highest possibilities in a spiritual sense. I knew whatever I undertook, I would be successful at it with the help and guidance of my Higher Power. I woke up from the dream feeling excited and filled with trust for what life had to offer.

A Notable Dream Key

Notice how you feel when you awaken from a dream. Write in your dream journal not only the elements and analysis of your dreams, but also your mood or emotional state immediately upon awakening. This is often a clue or a key to the hidden wisdom of your dream.

Analyze Dreams in Concert with Your Current Life Events

This dream occurred during a time of dramatic life change for me. When I dreamed of walking the steep path after the hurricane, I had just left my marriage—an investment of more than two decades in an abusive relationship.

The journey I embarked upon ultimately turned out to be starting my own counseling practice. From this, I would build skills with the tools I'd gathered, eventually sharing the results of my harvest with others. With the ax I'd be able to powerfully sever ties of the past as a victim. The hammer would help me construct and rebuild my life after the divorce. The knife represented cutting away past anger and resentments. The portable water jug was a cleansing symbol of spiritual renewal and survival. The rope symbolized learning to connect to my Higher Power while reining in the character flaws of my smaller self. The tool belt balances and centers my life from a position of strength.

I have grown in success and skills, taking the experience of cleaning up the aftermath of the dream hurricane and transforming it into tools to help others on their journey of self-discovery as they birth lives of more health, balance, and love.

Dreams of the Future and a New Way of Life

The following example illustrates a symbolic dream of the future and reassurance for adopting a new way of life. Three weeks after I left my marriage, I dreamed I was giving birth in a hospital. A doctor checked my progress, but I knew I was not yet ready to give birth. I left the hospital and returned home for a more natural birth. At home, an Indian woman put down two grass mats—one for my head and one for my body—in a shaded outdoor setting that reflected openness and freedom.

In the next year, this dream came to fruition as a major turning point. I birthed a new life when I graduated with a double master's degree in the sciences of Human Services and Mental Health Counseling. Instead of choosing a traditional hospital setting for my career, I decided to try pursuing alternative healing paths.

The dream I had about giving birth was a dream of healing for what I had experienced in my marriage. The Indian woman in the dream was a mentor or midwife, guiding my physical body back toward healing. If I hadn't had this kind of help inwardly, I believe I would have died from the sheer physical, mental and emotional traumas I had experienced.

Waking Dreams and Divine Protection

Often the most poignant dreams are the ones we receive when we're awake. Waking dreams involve unusual occurrences that seem to further highlight an incident in our lives. The elements of waking dreams are interpreted symbolically like the elements of a sleeping dream, to bring greater insight into what's happening in your life. Waking dreams messages can also provide divine protection, as shown in the following example.

Just after I left my marriage, I stayed at a friend's house until I could decide what to do. Her boyfriend, who had been practicing psychotherapy in another state, soon arrived. I didn't know it, but he wasn't licensed or qualified to practice psychotherapy *anywhere* at that time. He had created an experimental approach to therapy that wasn't based on any traditional therapeutic modalities. From the get-go, I was leery of him. He started asking me questions and even offered me his unsolicited opinion.

"You could go home," he suggested.

My eyes widened as my throat choked, and my lower jaw dropped slightly. I was confused and instantly felt a concrete wall erect itself in my gut against this unwanted advice. It was as if he had flippantly said, "Here's a quick fix for you today."

At that moment a loud thunder bolt broke the silence. We heard a crashing, splintering sound in an adjacent room and ran to see what happened.

A tree branch that overhung the roof had broken off and shattered the skylight. As I looked up at the remains of broken glass, I noticed the outline left by the break formed the shape of an angel with a broken wing. The boyfriend was distracted by the incident and went outside to assess the damage. Mercifully I was spared any more of his overt pressure.

"God damn it!" he yelped, and I saw him grabbed his finger in pain as he inadvertently cut himself on the glass.

The waking dream message here was clear and I soon moved to another friend's house. A therapist who is full of anger and advises returning to an abusive situation is derelict in responsible professional behavior. Later I realized any anger I had about leaving my husband would break me in a similar way that the branch broke the window

The way I chose to use my awareness in this situation (by interpreting it as a waking dream) gave me the wisdom to leave a crisis behind instead of getting more deeply mired within it or return to a bad situation. I chose to use this moment as an opportunity to learn more and grow more loving. This I know: life encounters strive to teach us more about loving—always.

There is an answer for every situation or question in the journey of your life. The only thing that holds us back from realizing these answers is our attitudes. Learn the value of recording your dreams. Make a short note about every dream you recall, whether it's a waking dream or a sleeping one.

Asking for and Receiving Golden Messages

An extension of the waking dream is the golden message. Answers to your problems or questions may come from other people in your waking hours during the day. Be on the lookout for these golden messages; your Higher Power can be subtly working through them, too.

Sometimes golden messages come from an article you're reading or a sentence or two from a radio announcer. You may meet someone at the store who says something that stands out in your mind. All these instances and the following story are examples of golden messages.

A Golden Message from God

A woman was stressed out due to her weight and out-of-control eating. The stress of these health concerns was just too much for her and she felt overwhelmed. Often she wrestled with where she was with her life during counseling sessions, feeling the pressure to change.

She thought a move might help. "Maybe a change in location could help me find my purpose in life and get me away from this bad situation." But every time she asked for a message from God, the only thing she received was, "Stay where you are."

One night, she awoke from a fitful sleep of tossing and turning. She decided to connect with her Higher Power for counsel. She practiced a visualization and contemplated, asking her Higher Power, "Every time I've asked, you tell me to stay where I am. If I am to stay, I need another message from you. I need even more encouragement because I feel so hopeless."

She wondered how to get back to sleep again without visiting the refrigerator. She glanced at the radio/tape player next to the bed and decided to listen to relaxation tapes for a while. She hoped the tapes would put her to sleep.

When she turned on the player, she inadvertently turned on the radio. The first words she heard were, "Are you waiting for a message from God? Stay tuned."

This caught her attention. The announcer gave an advertisement for a local church, then came back to the initial question as promised.

"Are you looking for a change? Here's a message from God to you: Bloom where you're planted. God wants you to stay right where you are. God has a plan for you right where you are."

What an incredible golden message!

Be Aware and Listen for the Next Step

One morning I wrote the following passage to my Higher Power in my journal: "Please show me what I am to do next. I feel too eager. How can I slow down and enjoy the present?"

That day's mail contained an organization newsletter with worldwide distribution. I took time to read it during lunch. During the course of reading it, several thoughts bubbled to the fore front of my consciousness about the requests I had posed in my journal that morning. The following golden messages occurred to me:

(1) You'll know the answer when the right spiritual experience is behind you.
(2) Everything comes in its natural course in due time.
(3) Relax and stop worrying about the next step for now.

I was surprised to find that connecting with these insights cleared the confusion from my mind. I began to perceive life more calmly from a much fresher perspective from then on.

Soul Knows Everything in Dream Time

At the highest levels of unity, Soul knows everything. If you want to bring this inner wisdom to your consciousness, try the following technique tonight.

Before going to sleep, take time to check in with your breathing, counting down from five to one. Tell yourself to let go or relax, and decide upon awakening you'll have an answer to what you want to know.

Then check in with your purpose symbol. Think of someone or something you love. Lightly hold that feeling of love in your heart. Now remember your favorite music or sound. Next conceive a favorite smell, and finally a favorite healthy taste. Finish by asking your Higher Power to help you find the answers during your dream time, and slip off to sleep, knowing in the morning you'll awaken refreshed. When you awaken, the answers will be in the forefront of your thoughts.

At the moment of slipping to or from sleep, your psyche is open to truth and in direct contact with it. It is at this point that you are most able to perceive answers. Immediately note them in your dream journal. Record any insights or changes that happen in the weeks to come.

The Power of Awareness and Control

Two keys that help you consistently reap quality wisdom from your dreams are your level of awareness and control of your attention. This means developing a focus for dreaming in your life.

The difference between scattered attention and concentrated attention can be compared to the power of a 40-watt light bulb and the precision of a medical-quality laser instrument. Some people have scattered attention when they seek counseling. They jump randomly from one subject to another.

Other people come for a little polishing on a specific problem. Their attention is laser-like in its approach. It is so powerful that they accomplish their goals quickly. Which kind of attention would you prefer to use for your purpose?

Ways to Develop More Focus

Practicing the exercises and techniques outlined in this book is one way to develop more focused attention. Most request that you look upward, to the center of your forehead, when you close your eyes before you begin the exercise. This helps concentrate your highest attention on the part of the brain where insight occurs—a good focal point for sharpening your attention to laser strength. Doing this while connecting to your Higher Power as you know it exponentially increases your focus and intent.

One further way you can implement the exercises in this book is to record them and then play them back softly as you fall asleep. That way they can leave gentle impressions, further preparing you for dreaming by focusing your mind before you sleep. Remember you are *not* your mind. Your mind is the tool you choose to sharpen to achieve more of what you want in your life.

Making Room for More in Your Life

The following exercise helps you explore a larger awareness of yourself as you make room for more possibilities in your life.

Have someone you trust read the following exercise/visualization to you or record it in advance on a tape cassette for your bedtime listening. As you listen to the exercise, let yourself go in creating a safe space to experience this larger awareness.

An Exercise to Experience a Larger Awareness

Close your eyes and gently look upward to the point where insight occurs in your brain. Gently notice your breathing. Let your breath relax you. Now conceive of a safe place for you. This can be anywhere on earth. Your safe place could be outdoors or indoors. Maybe it is near the ocean or in the mountains. Or maybe it is your bedroom. Invite the child you were long ago to join you. Ask your shoulders to let go and relax. Ask your jaw to let go and relax.

Again notice your breathing. Feel it as it comes in through your nose and down into your lungs. Gently send your breath into your belly. Notice how your belly expands.

Now check your feelings. Silently ask yourself, "What am I feeling now?" Ask yourself, "What was I feeling earlier today?" Ask yourself, "Do I have feelings about my future?"

Ask yourself, "Am I only my feelings?" Then ask yourself, "If I can know my feelings, then what else am I?"

Begin to ask for the cause of your feelings. Let the first thing pop into your mind. What happened before the feelings began? What happened after your feelings? Let this awareness be a part of your consciousness. Then let it go.

Ask yourself, "How is it I can be aware of the cause of my feelings?"

Begin to check in with your thoughts. Observe your thoughts as they go across the screen of your mind. Let this checking in with your thoughts be part of your consciousness. Ask yourself, "Am I more than my thoughts?"

Begin to notice sounds in the room where you are. Are the sounds outside? Now expand your awareness beyond the building you are in. Go outside with only your consciousness. Is it night or day? If it's daytime, make it night. Look around you. What do you see or sense? Maybe there are houses, buildings, parks, highways, rivers or the countryside. Now conceive of looking or sensing the whole area from a bird's eye view. See or sense the whole state. Now view the whole country. Ask yourself, "Am I viewing the whole?" See your family, friends or relatives in their everyday lives. Expand your consciousness to view the whole earth. Enjoy the experience.

See the whole solar system. See the earth revolving around the sun. See other planets revolving around the sun. Everything is in balance. Conceive of yourself existing in that balance.

Again notice your breathing. Feel it as it comes in your nose and down into your lungs. Expanding and contracting your lungs as you breathe. Ask yourself, "How do I know myself as consciousness? Am I more than my thoughts, feelings and body?"

Conceive of expanding yourself to two times your size, now three times your size. Ask yourself, "How do I feel and what do I think as I expand and become larger?" (Give yourself a moment to reflect on this.) Now be your current size again.

Ask yourself, "How do I feel now after being so large? How does this awareness affect my attitude about my present size?" Now conceive of yourself at your *perfect, balanced, realistic* weight.

What does your body feel like at this size? Hold that image of yourself lightly in your mind while remembering your purpose image or picture. Do this at least three times daily for three weeks and journal the results of your experience.

What moved you the most with this experience? Apply what moved you the most to your purpose. How can holding a larger awareness help you maintain a more balanced life?

Each time you do an exercise such as this, it builds creative muscles. Those creative muscles are keys to reaching a balanced diet and maintaining a balanced body through an expanded awareness.

Creativity and Imagination: Your Keys to Manifesting Change

Consider for a moment how creativity could be weight balance secret for success. Is creativity a mysterious quality only artists, writers, and performers have? Do you even need artistic talent to be creative?

Creativity is a God-given right of everyone. By accessing your creativity, you can do almost anything. To create is simply to bring something new into existence. Individuals use creativity to manifest change all the time.

Deep inside you have a natural urge to create and change as all things in the world do. That urge is a natural talent of Soul. Reading this book is a catalyst for creativity and making change happen.

So how do you become more creative? How can you apply creativity to your goal of deepening and sustaining your results?

The Creative Principle

Let's talk about the three aspects of the creative principle: *knowingness, intention, and imagination.* When you allow these three aspects to shape your thoughts, you choose creativity.

Knowingness is knowing something with all your heart. "I just know I'm ready to do this." If you *hope* or *wish* or *try* to do a thing, then you will fail. Thoughts of hoping and wishing are creating a lack of something and trying isn't really doing it. In other words, what you hope or wish for, your subconscious is hearing you don't have. What you try isn't done. Your attention is focused on lack.

Whatever you put your attention upon, you will get. So it is better to simply know it is yours or know you can do it. For example, instead of saying, "I wish I had better eating habits," (thinking from a lack of things) say, "I know I'm developing good eating habits." Then strive to align your actions with your words and make it true! See the difference?

Knowingness is not easy. In reality, knowingness has many saboteurs. The worst enemy of knowingness is opinion based on past fact. For example, an opinion based on past fact may say you have no creativity or will power. If your current beliefs are based on this, you'll sabotage yourself from the start. These assumptions are really only *past opinions.*

Change happens simply by starting with a different knowingness and then following through with it. Go ahead and do an exercise from this book to prove it to yourself.

A Simple Story about the Power of Intentional Dreaming

In 1986 I dreamed of living and working in a historic home on the St. Lucie River. It didn't make sense to me at that time because I was still married to my husband, but I wrote it down anyway and even made a sketch of the dream house.

Later I could not afford to buy a home like this because of past complications from the divorce. At first I believed such a millionaire's home was beyond my means. Yet I simply chose to trust my prayers and asked for the best location for my business and home while surrendering the outcome to God.

Ten years later, I found a historic home up for lease overlooking the expansive St. Lucie River. I looked at this opportunity as an earned blessing on many levels for many reasons.

Although leasing the mansion was still beyond my means, I brainstormed, negotiated, and generally impressed the landlady with what I had to offer the home and what a great tenant I would be. As the manager of her family trust, she could tell how much I loved this historic home and she knew that I would take the best of care with it. The details of how I came to lease this house are too numerous to list, but it was truly an amazing experience and an example of the power of creativity and intentional dreaming. It's a joy for me to share this haven for healing with others on the St. Lucie River.

Intention Is Simply Your Purpose

The aspect that helps you create is *intention.* Intention is simply your purpose which can be identified as "inner action." Remember when you use images, you're speaking the language of the subconscious mind and talking to the subconscious is dealing directly with 97 percent of your total mind.

The Shaping Force of Imagination

The third shaping aspect of creativity is *imagination.* When you know what you want, and you know it is possible and your intention is clear, *then you can imagine yourself doing it.* This is the reason why I ask you to specifically see yourself doing certain activities when you practice the exercises, techniques, and visualizations in this book.

For example, if you want to eat healthy foods to sustain your balanced weight (a logical conclusion), use your imagination to see, feel, and experience yourself eating healthy foods, maintaining your best balanced weight. This way, your inner pictures and feelings send clear messages to your mind that match your intention and purpose.

Matching the inner pictures with outer goals is crucial. The way to reach your goal, whether it is balancing your weight, your life, or feeling good about yourself, is by matching the force of your imagination with your intentions and purpose.

Using Imagination to Prepare a Contingency Plan

Another way to use the imagination for your success is to look ahead and take steps to correct any problems the future might bring to derail you. One example of this is to imagine arriving home from work. You're tired. This is a dangerous time because you can see yourself grabbing some fast foods. What can you do to prepare for this likelihood?

Imagine preparing food in advance. Then take time twice a week to prepare the nourishing whole foods you imagine in a way that they can be served quickly after a long workday. Use this imaginative technique to head off potential stumbling blocks in anything you do. This basic technique for empowerment is one way to be a dynamic for creativity in all aspects of your life.

Using Purpose, Intention, and Imagination for Exercising Made Easy

Find an outdoor passion you love. For example, I love to walk at night through the historic city with a friend and my dog. First is my purpose: walking for easy exercise. Second is my intention: "I know I'll do it." Third, I imagine and see myself walking—where, when and what time of day. Then I simply make myself do it until it becomes a habit (do it routinely for at least 21 consecutive days and it becomes easier to do it than *not* to do it).

I chose to know I could do it. Once the pattern is set, it becomes customary and easy for the body to do. Joy comes from following the pattern and looking forward to each walk as an adventure.

Strengthening Your Muscles for Active Creativity

Please note that if you have been passive for some time, passive activities easily become the most uncontrolled habits. The result is you become the effect of them. The most common passive habits are overeating, spending money and shopping, too much radio, television or movies.

In a balance these activities are okay, but too much results in your creative abilities becoming weak. Like physical muscles (which are dormant when healing a broken bone), your creative abilities have a tendency to atrophy, too. So start slowly with creative exercises and let them gradually build up your "creative muscles."

Making Things Happen with a Plan of Action

To maintain good results, form a plan of action. The first step is to *access the resources you have now.* For example, to slim down your thighs you might want to find someone who could give you instruction in the proper exercises.

Next, *imagine yourself having fun while exercising.* Imagine how you will look in a realistic way. Then, *imagine how you can maintain exercise as a part of your daily routine,* similar to brushing your teeth. Finally, *implement it.* This is the way to be a catalyst for creativity in loving yourself and changing your life.

Live Happily Forever After

> *The elements of dreams, creativity and imagination are spiritual first steps to birthing the life you need.*

Feel free to draw upon the techniques and exercises in this chapter whenever you need the upliftment and joy they can bring. It's important to play with these light, fun activities; they help show you the ebbs and flows that are a natural balance on any journey of life.

Low points do exist in the best of success stories. The greatest heroes inevitably reach complicated times of being stuck in negative feelings and pessimistic thought patterns. At times they deny themselves excitement and joy, or may feel unappreciated, threatened, or disconnected from life, without quite knowing why.

At these times, it's important to be gentle with yourself. In Chapter 8, you'll find ways to confront dark times and the shadows of life while rediscovering your hidden talents and strengths. Chapter 8 also reveals more than a dozen exercises to help you develop attitudes and acquire skills that keep you in balance as you further deepen and sustain your success.

Chapter 8
Anger, Denial and Resentment

The last chapter revealed deeper ways to manifest the life we dream through waking dreams, sleeping dreams, and dreams of the future. We explored ways to harness our energies and talents by using creativity and imagination. Now let's dispel the hidden reasons why some mental and emotional responses, such as frustration or fear, may continue to persist. This chapter covers ways to keep the shadow of their influence from further holding you back from your best future.

The Tinsmith's Escape

The Spiritual Dimension of the Enneagram: Nine Faces of the Soul by Sandra Maitri opens with a parable from the recently deceased Sufi teacher Indries Shah. It's about an unjustly imprisoned tinsmith who miraculously escapes from prison. The following synopsis tells the methods he used for escaping when asked about it years later.

> When the tinsmith was asked how he escaped, he replied that his wife (a weaver) had woven the design of the lock to his prison cell into the prayer rug upon which he prayed five times a day. He realized that the rug contained the lock design, so he struck a deal with his jailers to get tools to make small artifacts, which the jailers then sold for a profit. He surreptitiously used the tools to fashion a key, by which he eventually made his escape.

The moral of the story? Understanding the design of the lock that keeps us imprisoned can help us create the key that opens it.

Moving Past Blockages and Denial

Basically because the mind functions like a machine, experiences, facts, feelings, or beliefs that are unacceptable to it are routinely blocked out or denied. This happens in even the best of minds because the whole purpose of denial is to keep experiences, facts, feelings, or beliefs which would *most likely overwhelm or disrupt you* out of your everyday consciousness.

The Emotional Fallout That Precedes Destructive Patterns

People become overwhelmed most often when the worst of circumstances come into their lives. Upon reaching a state of overwhelm, they will tend to drop into hopeless or helpless states more easily. It's dangerous to remain in either of these states for any period of time because they often induce the destructive life patterns which were addressed in Chapter 7 (i.e. overeating, overspending, too much radio, television or movies).

Elizabeth Kubler-Ross' pioneering books on death and dying helped establish the modern hospice movement and brought to mass awareness the five stages that precede and give closure to the act of dying—(1) denial and isolation, (2) anger, (3) bargaining, (4) depression, and (5) acceptance.

Take note of these five stages. When people let go of preciously-held beliefs, many times they will pass through these same stages before reaching and accepting a new awareness. Often each loss, whether the death of a loved one, dropping an old belief, or releasing a limiting behavior pattern, needs to be grieved and honored in the natural process of the five stages before the individual can move to a higher level.

Sometimes dreams help facilitate the transition that begins with these five stages. At other times the exercises in this book can help. In certain cases a support system of friends who understand the process can offer assistance to you, as you would for them.

The ideal way to shift to new states of consciousness is to move alternately between the five stages in a random pattern that's comfortable for you, until you reach a state of acceptance gradually. It's imperative to avoid getting stuck in any one state for too long (which can bring on feelings of confusion or hopeless before you default to a destructive life pattern).

When you do feel confused, helpless, or hopeless, reach out to friends, a support group, or turn to the exercises and techniques in this book for help. Often it's just a matter of trying different tools, techniques, and support systems until you find a combination that works for you.

Stopping the Cycle of Destructive Patterns

A woman named Debbie wants to feel satisfied with eating more fresh vegetables and fruits in a balanced diet. Yet she is pulled back to old mental patterns and body habits, thinking she needs only meat and potatoes for satisfaction. In other words, she reacts as a victim of her thought patterns for meat and potatoes. At the time she thought this, she was overtired and her energy was down. When her energy gets low, she typically reacts from discouragement.

Given this situation, anyone would slip backward. When you're weak, it's relatively easy for an avalanche to occur. However, Debbie decided to be aware of her mental state and take responsibility to stop the slip. She connected with this book and friends again, both of whom successfully helped her to keep the slip from turning into an avalanche.

Freeing Yourself from the Bedrock of Destructive Patterns

When fears come up and bring with them your deepest worries and doubts, how do you usually react? Do you tend to isolate yourself and nurse your emotional state in a feedback loop of depression or guilt? Do you react with anger by lashing out at everyone closest to you—your family, friends, and co-workers? Or do you deny you're depressed, frustrated, or angry and eventually draw up a deal with the devil, bargaining away all your hard-earned weight balance success in exchange for eating habits designed to rocket your serotonin levels? Delving into the foundation reasons why these emotional states persist is the first step to permanently clearing them.

Beating Mind Games

The mind can take a warm memory and, in the short space of a minute, trick you into turning it into one that produces guilt or resentment. This is because memories and emotions are intricately linked in the mind.

One way to free yourself from their influence and move beyond them is to heal resentments of the past by exposing their shadow sides, then find one way to take the next small step. Using the techniques outlined in this chapter, my patients learn to let go of their resentments gradually, one by one.

I was amazed to find that even within myself many resentments grew, numerous as weeds in a driveway. A man rode by on his bicycle yesterday morning as I was weeding and called, "It's a never-ending job!" I agreed as he passed and continued weeding. But after he passed I found I no longer resented the job. Instead I chose to change my perspective and weed out of love for my home. What a different attitude to take! A changed outlook made the job a joy for me!

A Flash of Insight from the Past about Resentment and Guilt

I searched for more truth on the origin of my guilt feelings three years ago. Because I had spent several years exploring this in my quest for understanding, I got a flash of insight as I was reading an article on the many lifetimes that the priests of the day used guilt to imprint control over the masses. As I read this, I felt an intense, fiery pain, as if I was awash in waves of agony.

These waves were past rips and scars of how I bought into the guilt that was handed down from three or four generations of ministers in my maternal family history. Due to the strong influence guilt has had upon members of my family, I always bought into the feeling that I was never good enough. I also knew from this insight that if something in the past was implied or judged as wrong, I'd feel guilty about it.

After this insight, I built even stronger boundaries to protect my understanding of my true Self. As I felt stronger and stronger, I noticed that food began to taste better than ever and my eating habits improved. I started to deeply savor the flavors of foods in a similar way that a gourmand would. I was no longer driven by an unseen force to eat my way out of the "Land of Guilt." Gradually the guilt in my gut disappeared.

You can take the approach of savoring your meals like a gourmand too, simply by slowing down to completely enjoy every flavor and every moment of the experience. This will help you feel fuller sooner, discouraging you from eating until you're stuffed.

Sometimes it seems we must move mountains of resentments that have been handed down through the generations. Emotions of resentment, anger, guilt, doubt, or fear which are passed on to you second-hand from relatives are as destructive as a knife to the throat or poisonous acid eating away your peace of mind.

Understanding How We Adopt Family Shadows

Rejuvenation is defined as "to make young again." You can rejuvenate yourself and your current relationships when you strive to live more consciously with a balanced awareness of the legacy of your past generations.

Depending on personal family history, the cycles and dynamics within families bear fruit every fourth through sixth generation. When a family unit is tight, strong, and loving, the members of that family enjoy the strength of cohesiveness and support from familial love, which helps them ride through the hard times of the currents of life better.

However when a family unit is not close (antagonistic), or displays emotional fusion (lack of boundaries, poorly differentiated relationships), or is dysfunctional, then the family dynamic becomes more of a liability than an asset to its members. The more closed the family system is, the more rigid and automatic the family responses and patterns become. Family members who identify strongly with or idolize other members may be prone to continue destructive behavior patterns throughout generations.

How does this happen? Family behavior patterns can be passed along in stories, as well as through attitudes, liaisons and affinities between family members for generations. The intensity of these patterns often unconsciously pulls at our attention and influences our lives on a subconscious level. Sometimes they interfere with the ability to make wise, conscious, decisions and undermine the ability to live fully and function truthfully in the present modern world. One way to discern and understand your family dynamic is through a charting method known as the *genogram.*

The Genogram

A genogram is similar to a family tree in that it describes family relationships between its members. Primarily used by mental health experts, physicians, and clergy, a genogram maps biological processes (such as birth order, marriages, pregnancies, deaths, households, and other historical and medical events).

A genogram can also map the emotional dynamics in relationships between family members, such as whose relationship was conflict-ridden, which relationships were close, the incidence of physical abuse or incest, as well as other patterns of dysfunction within the family history for generations. When used effectively, this tool gives a "snapshot" of the historical and dynamic influences at work in a family. You can benefit from this information. Simply draw your own family genogram and use it to become more conscious of the hidden influences within your family.

The Genogram Survey

Draw up a history of your family in your journal, using circles to signify females and squares to delineate males. Record at least four generations of your family, beginning with your grandparents. Add each generation (your parents, their brothers and sisters, you and your brothers and sisters, your children and their cousins) and their spouses or significant others. Do your best to fill in the relationship dynamic by answering the following questions in the genogram survey.

(1) Label addictions such as alcoholism or drug abuse (recreational or over-the-counter).
(2) Note any medical information you can. Look for chronic illness, eating disorders, depression, or other mental health problems. Some health concerns you might be aware of are the following: allergies, arteriosclerosis, arthritis, asthma, cancer (what kind), cataracts, cystic fibrosis, diabetes, Down's syndrome, dwarfism, emphysema, epilepsy, heart disease or heart attack, hemophilia (or other blood disorders), hypertension, hepatitis (or other liver ailments), multiple sclerosis, muscular dystro-

phy, sickle-cell anemia, Tay-Sachs, and tuberculosis. Add any others that apply to your family that are not listed.

(3) Label any emotions that might define certain members or that they might be stuck in. For instance did you parents argue? Did you mother remain bitter? Did either of your parents experience loss and grief? If so, how did they teach you to handle it by their example? Did either parent have difficulty overcoming fears?

(4) Using straight lines, connect the relationships in your family which were loving and close. Which relatives do you identify with or idolize?

(5) Connect all the conflict-ridden relationships with jagged or wavy lines. How much of what you do today is directly or indirectly influenced by unresolved issues in these relationships?

(6) If possible, ask the family for more history. What were their lives like? How did their lives turn out? Successful or tragic? In what ways? As sensitively as possible, ask for specific details. What "family secrets" do members choose *not* to talk about? Fill out your chart accordingly.

Emotional History

In addition, answer the following questions to determine the past messages your family sent you. Understanding these things consciously takes them from being stumbling blocks and turns them into personal stepping stones out of unconscious behaviors.

(1) Ask yourself, what message or belief did my mother pass on to me?

(2) Ask yourself, what message or belief did my father pass on to me?

(3) Ask this same question for each grandparent, both maternal and paternal.

(4) Write each in a boxed area that relates to the relative on your genogram.

(5) Then reflect on background factors in your family that are always at work.

The emotional beliefs passed on to you by previous generations are powerful coercive forces that affect you and your choices in life. Knowing your family background can help you understand where some of your feelings and actions originate and allow you to make more conscious, satisfying, rewarding choices in the way you react or behave, tremendously effecting the course of the rest of your life.

Standard Symbols for Genograms

Symbols to Depict Family Membership and Structure:

Male: ☐   Female: ◯   Birth year: Death date:

Identified Person: (O)   Living together relationship or affair: ☐ ◯

Marriage date:

Martial separation give date: Divorce date:

Children: List in birth order with oldest on the left:

Fraternal twins: ◇◯   Stillbirth: ⊠   Members of current household circle them:

Identical twins: ◯◯   Abortion: Pregnancy: Miscarriage:

Foster child: Adopted child:

Symbols Denoting Interactional Patterns between People:

Close relationship: Very close or fused relationship: ≡≡≡

Distant relationship: — — — — —   Conflictual relationship: ∧∧∧∧

Fused & conflictual relationship: ⧚⧚⧚   Estangement or cut-off: —┤ ├—

Sexual abuse: ☐⤳◯

List addictions in the family.   Symbol is: ▬ ◖

List family losses:

Your Family History

This is your family history in a nutshell. It tells a lot about the tides of power and the relationship dynamics within your family, as well as your family resilience to dealing with stress and the cycles of life. It also shows behavior patterns and emotional choices that often repeat themselves, passed on from family members across generations. (Editor's note: For examples of famous family genograms, please refer to Monica McGoldrick's book *Genograms: Assessment and Intervention.* See Genogram drawing and legend on page 117.)

A Story of Accepting My Own Personal Shadows

Earlier in this chapter, you read about how my maternal grandfather and the men in the ministry in my family lineage spread guilt and fostered resentment through being overly judgmental. On the flip side is the story about the women on my paternal side of the family and the legacy they passed down to me. Both sides are pertinent to who I am today and reflect the double whammy that guilt and resentment has played in my life.

It's often easy to blame our mothers, believing they have slighted us in so many ways. After all, isn't it the mother who stereotypically provides unconditional, nurturing love? This nurturing is the wellspring that supplies both a basis for self-worth and acceptance of others. Mothers who use their feminine creative energy for birthing, sustaining, and nurturing their offspring epitomize this ideal.

I was totally astonished to discover that my paternal grandmother and great-grandmother had much more influence on my self-worth and acceptance of others in this regard.

In the beginning of the 1890s, my paternal grandmother and her younger brother were abandoned by their mother on the steps of an orphanage. Her mother told the nuns that she would return for her children.

In the late 1950s, my grandmother discovered her mother had said this and that she eventually *did* return to claim her children, but by the time she did, it was too late. My grandmother and her brother had been separated and adopted with no traceable records long before that.

I can only imagine the trauma my grandmother must have felt from first being separated from her mother and then her younger brother. I feel empathy for what she must have gone through at the age of five in coming to terms with this tremendous loss and its associated grief.

Later on my grandmother married and gave birth to a child—my father. Although she became pregnant a second time, the family secret is that she used a coat hanger to induce premature labor and consequently aborted that child.

My father married my mother and she gave birth to my older brother. Three years later my mother became pregnant with me. At that time my grandmother's beliefs strongly influenced my father's insistence that I too, should be aborted. Living in close proximity to my father's parents, my mother succumbed to their influence and set up an appointment for the abortion.

My mother has told me this story several times, so much so that it is engraved upon my heart. She was on the table about to undergo the procedure when the doctor arrived wearing a bloody apron. Terrified that he was going to butcher her, my mother jumped up and ran out of the room in tears.

The source of the guilt and abandonment I felt for most of my life sprang from my mother and the emotions I experienced through her as a fetus. I had a direct link to the emotions she struggled with during her pregnancy with me. For most of my life I deeply resented and hated my mother for the legacy of this emotional backlash.

I didn't realize until much later that the self-hate and rejection I felt originally stemmed from my paternal great-grandmother's action of abandoning her children. Everything started with that single, long-ago abandonment. Beliefs and attitudes are primarily based on feelings and the illogic children sometimes use to rationalize things to themselves (such as feeling worthless, thinking that boys have more value than girls) or to blame themselves, as if they somehow could have done something different to change the outcome.

I have vivid memories of visiting my grandparents as a child. After returning home, I'd ask my mother, "Why doesn't Grandma ever talk to me? She just tells me to go lie down and take a nap."

I always felt she loved my older brother so much and that I was unimportant and unacceptable to her. I always tried so hard to please everyone, yet I felt such unresolved guilt.

What had I done? It must have been something terrible. I concluded, "It's all my fault," as any child would. Only compulsive eating patterns gave a clue to the unbalanced state and constantly striving for control that I felt (which existed within me constantly from as early as six years old).

Throughout my life I experienced repeated losses, as if I were caught in a never-ending grieving process, in much the same manner as the Sisyphus myth (of rolling the stone up the hill, only to have it roll back down, endlessly repeating this cycle, again and again). Perhaps you've experienced similar endless cycles.

I know I enacted cycles of loss and abandonment within myself continuously, buying into the myth of *Dieting Will Give Me Self Esteem and Acceptance,* until I learned the lessons contained in this book. Isn't it better to make these cycles conscious, in order to face and overcome them than to allow them to stay subconscious while you endlessly repeat the cycles? I overcame my belief in these myths. You can do it, too.

Discovering Your Shadow Side

Like Alice in Wonderland, you might be ready to go down the rabbit hole and explore more about the shadow side of your feelings and the memories connected with them. Uncovering the deeper personal reasons why these cycles continue to persist in your life may be the first step to change.

The White Rabbit Technique

Here's an exercise to try. Imagine that, like Alice, you have dived into the darkness of the rabbit hole. At the bottom you'll find your favorite fears and worries, those you continually pull out from time to time. What do you think, feel, or say to yourself *from the shadow side?* Write about what your fears and worries have to say to you in your journal. Strive to know them objectively. Ask, "Why are you in my life?" and "What wisdom do you have to share with me?" Write down their answers in your journal.

What I've found is that each problem or worry in life actually has a gift for you, once you learn to perceive it. Ask each fear or worry, "What gift or personal strength are you trying to bring to my attention? What do I need to develop more of in order to balance and bring this fear or worry to normal size?"

Make an effort to mock up feeling the personal strength which will balance your problem or weakness. For instance, if you feel threatened or fearful, ask your Higher Power, "How can I feel more brave?" Then choose to feel brave. See what happens. Choose to use the imaginative capacity you have and, like Alice in Wonderland, feel big, strong, and brave.

Living in a Sea of Experience with the Influence of Your Higher Power

This sea of substance is forever alive and active. It is sensitive beyond our mind's wildest dreams or imaginings. The thought pictures of the mind can mold this substance into expression.

Ask yourself, "How can I choose to see things in a more amusing way? How can I be more trusting of my process? How can I choose to be excited about new changes?"

Then take the words and say, "I am choosing to be amused. I'm choosing to be excited more and more. I am choosing to trust in positive outcomes."

What you give out is what you get back. It's time to let go of the past. What could stop you now? Only the hostility you harbor inside your own heart.

Turning Anger or Primal Rage into Energy that Works for You

Does your anger strike you as being like a burning coal? Or do you just end up confused and hurt without understanding? What can you do about this? By knowing the heart of your anger better, you can become free.

The Heart of Resentment and Rage

The illusion at the heart of rage, denial, and resentment is that you can exert control over people, places, and events in your world when in reality you have *no control* over anything outside of yourself.

This faulty impression about power and control comes from the small self—the ego. Believing in this only keeps you confused, frustrated, and disappointed. Confusion is another word for resenting yourself, resenting the flow of life, and resenting the choices you've made in the past, which were dictated by past shadows.

Confusion and resentment lead to frustration, hostility, and stress—attitudes that release bodily manufactured chemicals (such as the steroid hormones of adrenaline and cortisol) and propagate them through the body, creating emotional level addictions within your body to those chemical reactions. (The stress hormone cortisol has also been known to lead to carbohydrate cravings and overeating, as well as abdominal fat).

Your mind and emotions may dislike what's going on, but your body is driven to seek out life situations and replay personal interactions with people, places, and things that stimulate the release of the body chemicals to which it is physically addicted. This theory forms the basis of Stress Pattern Processing.

Indulging emotional level addictions over time speeds biological aging, debilitates your immune system, and leads to disordered eating habits. It's fairly well-accepted that long-held stress from destructive attitudes (resentment, guilt, and anger) are actually precursors for cancerous conditions that develop later in life.

Be aware! Take charge of those things which you *do* control! Time to change old thinking and feeling patterns—time to reveal another layer of your true self hidden in the shadows of your dark side.

Hidden Rage

Hidden rage frequently elevates itself in order to be noticed, often expanding to many times its actual size. Many shadow traits you may have ignored, disavowed, or disowned over the years will do this in order to get your attention. The traits that you may considered your worst often have a "positive side" that's just begging for acknowledgment. When you embrace your rage and realize all the good qualities it has to offer you on the flip side, it reduces in size and nature, allowing you to manifest it in appropriate amounts in suitable situations. In many cases, rage becomes normal anger and no longer controls you—you manage it.

Rage can be hidden so consider this: did you have temper tantrums when you were young? Ask, "In what ways did I get angry when I was a toddler?" Rage is so undercover for most people that they can't acknowledge how much of a hold it has over their lives.

Remember repressed anger turns into guilt, self-loathing and self-hate. It may take months, years, or a lifetime but eventually repressed emotions will turn self-destructive. Some people spend a lifetime coming to this conclusion, but you can choose to understand it right now. You are worth whatever it takes to get it.

Feel good about yourself right now. Feel good that you've come this far. Ask yourself, "Do I want to move forward and be free?" If so, say aloud, "I choose to be willing to do whatever it takes to be free."

Embracing the Heart of Rage

Take the same exercise as before and go down the rabbit hole to meet your rage. Ask, "What wisdom do you have to share with me?" Write down the answer in your journal.

Ask your rage, "What gift or strength are you trying to bring to my attention? What do I need to acknowledge or what positive aspects come with the gifts that rage brings me?" Write down what you receive. Acknowledge, honor and embrace the positive gifts you find in the shadow of your rage.

Write a Poem About Anger

Another simple tool to use to expel repressed anger or resentment is to write an anger poem. The following poem is an example of anger being expressed instead of repressed. When you read the poem, listen to the compassion and courage Sally used in confessing her heartfelt anger. When you are finished, write a poem about a strong emotion that you experienced this week. Here's one example.

The Great Debate

by Sally G.
I am so irate because I hate to work late and since I don't rate,
It is my fate and my joy to be and love a reprobate.
When I ate and ate nothing would sate my appetite, so my weight

Kept growing, turning away my bedmate, which would exacerbate/exaggerate,

The situation so I needed to placate my anxiety and quiet the great debate

In my mind and allocate my energy if I quit lying prostrate

And not gestate or stagnate and endlessly berate.

Myself as I have in the past so I must not hesitate

To right away activate an exercise plan with my housemate

And not complicate it by issuing a mandate

Too immense and great that I would immediately deviate

From any plan to help me re-create

My mind and body because I want to medicate myself and not tolerate

Life on life's terms, and obliterate the world around me, hoping to terminate

All thoughts and actions to rehabilitate me. So I don't want to participate

In anything, but just vegetate and hibernate.

Take a Divine Shower—-A Simple Technique for Disengaging from Anger

For many years Lorraine loved her husband and family life. She was proud of the fact that she wed such a successful man. After many years of marriage, Lorraine developed an intense dislike for her husband as he did for her. Lorraine began to eat to stuff her anger. She gained over eighty pounds.

As time went by, these feelings grew into a rage, the likes of which she had never before experienced. She couldn't understand why she felt so enraged whenever her husband said or did anything. Although her husband had addictive problems and she had eating problems, they still remained married.

Through spiritual study, Lorraine learned about the Law of Cause and Effect (karma). In her dreams, Lorraine became aware that she had been instrumental in destroying her husband's character and marriage in a past life. As a result, both of them had created a spiritual debt for this lifetime. She saw this situation as an opportunity to pay off that debt.

However, even though she was aware of this, she was too emotional to sustain this higher awareness. She tried to let it go, to give it to God. She would say, "I turn this over to you, God." Yet she always took it back the next time she thought of her husband.

Lorraine decided to attend a spiritual seminar. Knowing that she always felt divine love at these seminars, she was eager to go. She asked her Higher Power to show her a technique to use to let go of the anger she felt toward her husband.

At the seminar she learned about a Divine Shower Technique. She practiced it each morning before the day began. While she showered, she sang the word

HU, which is an ancient prayer song to God. Then she imagined the Holy Spirit pouring thousands of shimmering stars over her, showering her from head to toe with the divine love of God.

Lorraine explained to me that the water became for her the love of the Holy Spirit. The most peaceful feeling overtook her in these moments, cleansing her of inner and outer anger and frustration. She sensed anger flowing out of her body, out each fingertip, spiraling down the drain. She continued with her daily life, beaming with joy and love for all of life. She let go of her animosity and stopped reacting to her husband.

"This wasn't always easy," explained Lorraine. "Some days my Divine Shower was quickly forgotten and I'd enter conversations with my husband and soon we were stuck in another angry confrontation. However, I continued to do this technique every day. Little by little, I gained more control of my emotions."

Lorraine also realized that as she surrendered this anger more and more to her Higher Power, an inner healing was taking place, so gradually that she barely noticed. Her attitude was changing—and so was her husband's.

Eventually she was able to give her husband unconditional love, even laugh at his jokes, and once again he could smile at her. To her surprise, the extra weight she had gained started to drop off naturally and gradually.

Soon they were both on friendly terms. During this time, they both realized it was best to move on with their lives without each other. Lorraine knew in her heart that the karmic debt (of destroying his character and marriage in a past life) had been balanced, repaid, and eventually put to rest, totally resolved. She was grateful for the experience and at peace with the outcome.

Seeds of Doubt

The seeds of doubt are all around us continually. Do you want to see the vision of yourself that disparages you or do you choose to see a person who acknowledges and boosts your self-esteem?

Linda had deep-seated doubts about her worthiness. She used a visual technique to help clear the self-doubt that plagued her for this lifetime. It took a long time for Linda to isolate self-doubt as a major contributor to her need for therapy over the years, but this discovery gave Linda the opportunity to use the following technique to finally clear it.

Visual Picturing Technique

(1) Linda asked herself, "What does this self-doubt and self-punishment look like?" She pictured a pioneer wagon stuck in two deep ruts. Then she focused on the symbol for her purpose image.

(2) Next she closed her eyes and looked up at the center of her forehead where insight occurs within the brain. She asked her Higher Power to help her with her tendency to get caught in attitudes of self-doubt and self-blame. She asked for this symbol (that resembled a wagon stuck in two ruts) to change positively. She watched it change. She took her time with this technique and kept asking it to change positively.

When Linda tried this exercise, she saw a figure get out of the wagon and ask for more help. Three more people arrived and helped lift the back of the wagon. Then they lifted the front of the wagon so it could turn in a new direction.

Linda went about her life, but afterward she was transformed by this inner experience. She had turned a corner. The experience was so deep that Linda continued to have fresh insights about it for the next six months.

Are you plagued by doubts? Imagine an image that symbolizes your doubt. Then kick that symbol (in the metaphorical butt) and laugh.

Freedom is being able to be you and to love yourself as you are now. The rest of your dreams will come true as you start loving yourself more.

Confronting the Shadow Cynic

What could stop you now? Only *not recognizing* the Shadow Cynic within yourself. A cynic is someone who denies the sincerity of other's motives and actions. A cynic sneers or is sarcastic about people and life in general.

What is behind sarcasm? Do you know of anyone who automatically comes to mind (by their actions and attitudes) when you think of what it is to be sarcastic? Stand back and get a better look at this person. If you know their background, you may see that they survived a tough trauma while growing up. Trauma continues to exist within a person's subconscious mind in the way he or she views the world. Their perception of reality as seen through the lens of trauma is, most simply, a hostile one.

In fact, all information coming into a traumatized person's mind goes first through the mental filter of the mind's programmed hostility response. Then they judge the world as being insincere through their mental lens of hostility. Nothing can get past this filter until they first consciously choose to willingly surrender their old beliefs, attitudes, and actions.

So often we equate surrender with defeat. It's a common human response, a battle that has been fought all our lives where we're always trying to win something that was lost long ago (when the trauma was first initiated). However, you can choose to look at surrender not as defeat, but as *doing things differently*.

If you've been doing things one way all your life and you're still unhappy, why not try something different? The imagination is wonderful in that it can free us from our limitations and inhibitions, and lead to more freedom with body images.

Four Techniques to Stay Clear on Your Inner Body Image

The following techniques work easily and with efficiency. Suspend your disbelief and trust the process. Just follow the directions and try each exercise in the order given. Each one builds on the results of the one before, working in concert to help you attain your purpose.

Loading Your Ship Technique

Imagine giving up everything that's holding you back in your world. Give up old patterns of self-pity, anger at yourself or the world, or thinking you have to do everything for everyone. Make a fantasy of constructing a ship. After it is built, the captain directs you to load it up with all your old baggage, the stuff that weighs you down in the past or present. Thank the crew and captain for their help. Then wave good-bye to it from the dock and see it sail away.

You may do this as often as necessary to keep releasing feelings that drive you to hopelessness. Trust and keep doing it. You are worth the effort to get free.

Where Am I Right Now Technique

Take out a drawing marker or pen. In a drawing, answer the question, "Where am I right now?" This is not about art. Draw whatever first comes to mind, even if it is just stick figures. Then, give the drawing a voice by writing the following sentences and completing them.

The three sentences begin the same. "I am . . . I am . . . I am . . . ."

Now, journal as if you are talking to your best friend, explaining how you felt when you were drawing. Open your awareness like a wide river to the sea, and stay with the experience without having to have all the answers right now.

Bottoming Out Technique

In a second drawing, answer the question, "What is blocking me?" Use symbols, colors, shapes, textures, and lines in whatever way you like. Give yourself permission to dare to draw any way and anything you want. Give the drawing a voice and complete the following sentences, "I am . . . I am . . . I am . . . ."

Free Your Attitude Technique

Here's how you determine if an attitude you have grown up with works for you. Ask yourself the following questions. No second-guessing. Again let the first answer pop into your mind and write it down.

(1) Write your intent or purpose.

(2) Write your limiting beliefs. For example, "I have to think before take action and get active for my health." (This thinking will talk you out of taking action.) Or "I have to feel anxious to get motivated." Or another belief is, "I need to know 'why' before I can let it go!" Or "It's no good, I'll never be able to do it." Write down all your strong attitudes and limiting beliefs.

(3) Ask yourself to be willing to suspend your disbelief for now while you use this technique. (If you don't have the willingness or intent, the exercise is assured to fail.) Get honest and find your willingness.

(4) Imagine you have written this statement in the hardest material or substance known to man. What is it? A brick wall, a granite cliff, or a huge boulder. Whatever it is, see it.

(5) Sense the attitude or belief carved in the substance. How is it carved? How big are the letters? Do the letters have a color? In what font or typeface are the letters written?

Now answer either Yes or No to the following four questions.

(1) Does this attitude or belief produce *positive, joyful feelings or actions* for you on your way to your purpose?

(2) Does this attitude or belief take you *towards your purpose?*

(3) Does this attitude or belief have value in leading you *to your purpose?*

(4) Is this attitude or belief pertinent to *where you want to go* in your purpose statement?

I'll bet all the answers are no. If these beliefs were working, you wouldn't be reading this book. If you have trouble getting clear with this technique, share it with a trusted friend. Do this again and again for all your limiting beliefs.

Next, ask your Higher Power to help you see the carved belief change positively. Watch it change with your eyes closed as you focus on the center point just above your eyes where insight occurs in the brain. Sense it and allow it to change while giving yourself some time to do this. You can work with a partner or do this as a silent contemplation for healing.

Watch it change for several minutes, keeping your eyes closed. Keep asking it to change positively as you just watch. Any slight change is good. It may need to get worse before you understand that it is changing for the better. Do this several times during the week. Change either the stone or the message, whichever works for you.

"I've Got You, Babe" Surrender Technique

Cut out magazine pictures of images or symbols that have hypnotized or bound you in the past. Be aware of how these pictures have shaped your desires to look or be like a favorite actress or model. Make a collage of all the pictures you can find.

Now stand back and see what has "got you, babe" from the past. Finally take this collage outside and set it on fire. Let it go. All the while, ask your Higher Power to help you be free of those hypnotizing body images. Let it go!

Release Fear on the Way to Healing

This exercise is for healing tension and extreme stress for the mind, body, and will. For a reference point, the color red is used to strengthen the life force of the body and to give self-confidence to the mind and will.

Close your eyes. Say, "I love my Higher Power. I love Spirit. I love God." Imagine seeing all your past worst stresses rolled into the image of a huge gray cloud. The cloud is filled with all your fears, terrors, and worries. The cloud follows you as you hurry away. You enter a forest. All the while you know that God is near you always.

Now imagine you hear a soft inner sound. Surrender and trust that you can creatively follow that inner sound as it threads through the forest. Soon you come to a huge cement building. It's got an open entranceway with two twin pillars on each side. You walk in, still following the inner sound.

Next you enter a bathing area. Proceed to wash yourself under a gently falling waterfall. In this refreshing shower, you release all stress and fear. Imagine the stress pouring away from you.

As you step out of this cleansing area, someone safe drapes a Red Cloak of Consciousness around you. This renews your will, life force, and your mental strength. This image of this cloak can be used as a tool for further healing you as Soul.

The Mystery of Dying to the Old

The mystery of dying to the old begins with exposing the dark energy of your anger, your fears, your resentments, and surrendering all these aspects of yourself. This emptying time gives you the opportunity to strengthen your inner balance. Letting go of the old makes room for the new.

Let go of being seduced by the ways of old habits and allow the new energy of upliftment to shine like the morning sunrise after a dark, stormy night. Trust that the new energy will be available. The sun always rises and so do you.

Vision Quest

Nicki, a dark-haired, fragile-looking woman, has a history of repressed anger and aggression. Her years of bingeing, over-exercising, and starvation diets lead her to look for ways to break free. A therapist recommended that she sign up for a week-long workshop retreat in the Black Mountains of North Carolina.

One outstanding part of this workshop was the use of a vision quest as a way to break free of old habits. The initial assignment was to collect things that represent everything in your life that was shamed, rejected, or used to blame or betray you. Nicki put these symbolic shadow items in a black bag to show how she kept these parts of herself hidden from herself, where she thought no one else could see them.

Nicki found a variety of items and a symbolic meaning she attribute to each one. In her journal Nicki wrote the following passage with her list, which follows: "In all respect and humble reverence for the reality of life and ego, I choose to purify my memories and free myself from any attachments in my mind, emotions, and body. I release what is no longer a way of life for me. I gladly give up tokens of the old as I make room for new awareness as the Soul that I am."

(1) Death Symbol—a fallen leaf, crumbling after finishing its creative cycle, will transform into fertile soil, nourishing new growth over time

(2) "Why" symbol—a dried-up branch shaped like a 'Y' that represents forever asking "Why?" I never got an answer to this constant question, only more confusion

(3) Illumination Symbol—a stone with a face on it that looked like its crown chakra was opened represented 'weird-crazy' label. The gift of being 'weird' is really visionary

(4) Surrender Symbols—twelve seed pods represent the secret ways to surrender on the way to freedom

(5) Dream-Not-Planted Symbol—an acorn. Aspects of life put on hold

(6) Symbol of Openness—an exquisite fluttering butterfly came to rest and spread its wings in all its beauty, sharing beauty without an ounce of shame

(7) Symbol of Illusions—a pink mushroom hidden under a leaf spoke to me through my intuition, as I remembered a line from Alice in Wonderland

(8) Symbol of the Fall—a yellow leaf reminds me of the contemplating Soul and wanting to travel to the stars and breathe in the beauty of God

(9) Symbol of the Void—a totally black, shiny pod from the stream that reminded me that I am always drawn to understand the void

(10) Symbol of Rejection—a discarded bubble gum wrapper

The Surrender Ritual

The next part of the ritual involved letting go. At the evening bonfire, a white-haired, spry old man began to play a trance-like rhythm on the drums. Nicki's turn came. As she slowly stood before the group of twenty, she felt powerful. She addressed the fire: "I give up my attachments, one by one, to be purified and dispersed to the winds of change." The fire sparked and smoke curled up into space and time.

"I give up my anger at myself for being judgmental when I am a beautiful Soul."

"I freely give up anger and sadness at my life choices, for they are meant to be."

"I give up my anger and release its habit of catching my attention, telling me what's not fair and what's wrong, rather than what is good."

The drum thundered its response.

"I give up my anger to rest in the arms of the essence of life as it is."

"I give up my anger at wanting to understand the lessons I've learned." Nicki threw this symbol as hard as she could into the leaping flames.

"I give up wanting to understand with my mind. I choose to trust it to be."

"In all of this I respect with humble reverence the process of purifying my memories and freeing myself."

"This copy of my marriage certificate symbolizes love/hate and pain/pleasure and something that is no longer. I close the debt as I burn this copy in neutral divine action."

Nicki originally gathered the symbols for the bonfire to facilitate sharing her shadow story with the group at the communal gathering. She compiled a medicine bag that contained these symbols so she could carry the power of the wisdom that she had gained with her. Some of the older, out-dated symbols that she wanted to divest herself of were burned in the fire. These were things she no longer needed in her life.

You can choose to experience the freedom of this exercise for yourself. Gather your shadow symbols for a vision quest. Create it with several others or by yourself, the way you want it to be.

Prepare for Opportunity Disguised As Loss

The process of surrender is not a lesson in loss as much as it's an opportunity in disguise. Here are four "how-to" clues on navigating the process of surrender.

(1) Ask for an experience to learn surrender

(2) Be open to opportunity

(3) Be willing to surrender all that is holding you back

(4) Have patience and the conviction in your beliefs, knowing this will transpire with time.

Looking at Loss as an Opportunity to Make Room for the New

When you get caught in a series of losses you may tend to start to look at life as a victim. You might become machine-like in your automatic thoughts and habitual actions. This is slavery to the negativity of the mind. Continue to take positive actions and be sure to ask for help, if you need it.

When I faced my deepest shadows, I found losses accompanied my deepest fears. Those losses read like a dirty laundry list of life messes. The losses included my marriage, my oldest daughter, my ten-acre dressage center, three show horses, my dog and four cats, and my financial base. A few years later, I faced the loss of my sense of safety due to a stalker, loss of face when I had to file a restraining order and appear in the state attorney general's office. Four court appearances later resulted in a prison term for the offender, finally re-establishing my safety.

Yet these losses were hidden opportunities.

Higher Power knew I needed to face my gravest fears in order to put them to rest forever.

What I received in the way of gifts by going through those devastating losses were the deepest strength and freedom I have ever known. These spiritual qualities of strength and wisdom abide in me today and I share it with whomever I contact. The culmination of these experiences opened my heart in a way that wasn't possible previously. I couldn't have gained these riches of spirit in any other way than to go through the experiences I did. It was well worth it!

Chapter 9 explores the companion to the shadow side—a way to true balance. By learning more about how to embody the elusive qualities of forgiveness, gratitude, and grace, you'll take the next step toward embracing true freedom.

Chapter 9
Forgiveness, Gratitude and Grace

Accepting the Full Magnitude of Life

> *Understanding and accepting the full magnitude of life, both the shadow
> and its flip side, brings true balance.*

Chapter 8 revealed how shadows of anger, denial, and resentment limit life whenever they rule. It also highlighted how processing and releasing shadows makes room for new ways of being. The next step to living a life of more freedom is fully understanding and adopting spiritual qualities of forgiveness, gratitude, and grace.

Forgiveness---The Most Misunderstood Quality

Often people believe forgiveness implies full *exoneration* meaning "to relieve of responsibility," suggesting that alleged offenders are fully vindicated and not accountable. Nothing could be further from the truth. [Editor's note: Definition from *Webster's Ninth Collegiate Dictionary*, Private Library edition.]

In the world in which we live where the laws of physics rule, *every action begets an equal and opposite reaction.* In other words, the Law of Karma governs. However, the ultimate time, place and price of karmic debt against others (in word, thought or deed) is a divine decision, one that's weighed in a court where the scales of justice are exquisitely balanced and completely free from the taint of error or perjury.

Forgiveness---The Gift You Give Yourself

Forgiveness doesn't need two or more participants. Forgiveness doesn't need witnesses. It doesn't need to make an outward appearance. Forgiveness isn't interested in the outcome, retribution, recompense, or revenge. *True forgiveness* means "to cease to feel resentment against (an offender)."

All forgiveness takes is *you*—and a changed attitude.

Forgiveness primarily revolves around a changed consciousness, a changed heart. Fully and unconditionally forgiving others can make all the difference in the world to your life.

As difficult as it may seem, the skill to *truly forgive* everyone who has done wrong against you is a valuable one to develop. By fully releasing everyone involved in situations from blame, you'll have the key to keeping resentment out of your heart. This is the greatest gift you can ever give yourself—a life free from the emotional fallout of your own aggression.

A Story of Forgiveness

As I floated in a Florida pool one heavenly winter day, I found myself thinking in an expansive way. I reached inside my consciousness, wanting to find the cause of some chronic shoulder pain. What I found was leftover resentments in my consciousness towards a surgeon for mistakes that I thought he'd made during an operation. (He was supposed to do it perfectly and I always suspected that he didn't.)

I decided to try this forgiveness technique, so I focused on letting go of feelings of resentment and forgiving him fully. As I did, my shoulder freed. Then I began forgiving each person involved in the operation. Not that I haven't forgiven them for this situation a hundred times before. But the mind has a curious way of taking resentment back.

This time, as I forgave each person with all the love in my heart, my shoulder began to release even more. I floated more buoyantly in the water as I did this. I was in ecstasy.

Then I forgave myself for any role I might have played in the situation. I accepted the current state of things today as the way they are meant to be.

I accepted myself in my current condition and realized that whatever had happened, the experience was what I needed to become the person I am today—the person who will be able to complete my life's work on earth. I know that what is *now* is what is divinely meant to be.

During the next few months, I watched for ways this change of consciousness affected my life. I found that the more I accepted myself this way, the more my body began to change in appearance. At times I truly felt like a goddess. All previous self-images which were tied into societal beliefs about what is popular today were gone. Forgiveness is a powerful tool for shaping the body from the inside out.

Floating in a Pool of Forgiveness Technique

Try this forgiveness technique out for yourself the next time you have an opportunity to float in water or *now*. Lay on your bed and imagine you're floating in the most warm wonderful ocean of forgiveness—an ocean of love and mercy. Recall situations you would like to forgive. Fully forgive everyone involved and forgive yourself for your part in it. Finally, accept the current way things are today as the way they are meant to be—part of the Divine Plan. Practice this technique until it becomes a part of you.

Are You Ready to Forgive?

So often the forgiveness technique is put aside because people are just not ready to forgive. However, forgiveness is integral to healing, becoming whole, and taking back all your energy that is tied up in the emotions that go with *not forgiving.*

If you are not ready, know that when you reach a point of being tired of all the sadness in your life, or the addiction to food, relationships, shopping, or media consumption, then you will be ready to accept the gift of forgiveness.

Be watchful for the quick fix. Be careful of anyone who says, "I can make that better for you in one or two sessions," or any other quick-fix scenario. Fast ways are not always permanent ways. Wouldn't you rather address things permanently with a mended heart? Quick fixes seldom give you feelings of empowerment, such as, "I did this myself. I did the work and now the solution is permanently imprinted in my heart for all time."

Forgiveness Like a Mantra

I took another step and practiced a forgiveness technique with a friend I have known for 19 years. I shared a variation of the forgiveness technique with her over some herb tea. First I said, "I accept you for who you are."

Then I stated, "I forgive you for whatever you have thought, said, or done in this lifetime and all past lifetimes." Third I added, "I forgive myself for all I've thought, said, or done in this lifetime and all past lifetimes." Finally I said, "I send you spiritual love and I accept spiritual love."

I told her that I had been saying these forgiveness statements every day, even several times a day. I really wanted to let it all go. Yet, I added with a frown, "It seems like I'll be saying these statements like a mantra for the rest of my life!"

"I know," she said. We had a good laugh over that.

What I found is that doing the forgiveness technique like a mantra helped me open my heart in gentle waves of bliss and purity until I *got it* in a way that can't ever be taken away from me. This is the most precious gift.

Visualization and Progressive Relaxation to Shape the Body

Make a recording of the following script in a slow, relaxed voice. Then play the recording for yourself each night as you go to sleep. If you feel you can never relax, tell yourself, "Please do not relax. Simply enjoy listening to my voice" at the beginning of the recording. Start your recording with the following paragraph.

State your purpose with your symbol. Take three deep belly breaths and tell yourself, it is safe to relax. Close your eyes and conceive of a safe place. This safe place can be real or imaginary.

Look around your safe place and notice details. What sounds do you hear? What can you reach out and touch? Feel the texture of whatever you are touching. This is your safe place where you can go to lower your fears or anxieties.

Accept in your mind this visualization is not about trying to relax—just allow it to happen. Know you are safe. You can hold on as much as you like or you can let go and relax—deeply relax. That's right.

Let your hands rest easily in your lap, at your sides, or on the arms of your chair. Close your eyes, and think of your whole body growing limp and relaxed.

Accept in your mind that the muscles in the scalp and forehead are growing comfortable and relaxed. You may find that as you think of these muscles relaxing, they will.

As the muscles of the forehead relax you may notice a slight increase in tension around the eyebrows. Concentrate on the eyebrows and all around the eye and this tension will fade away. Accept in your mind the tiny muscles of the eyelids relax. Let the relaxation move deep inside the eyes and deep in back of the eyes.

Let all the facial muscles relax; over the cheekbones and the cheeks, the jaw and chin, the lips and mouth—all relax. The relaxation moves deep inside the mouth. As the muscles of the mouth relax, you may find that your mouth automatically becomes not too moist and not too dry, but just moist enough to keep you perfectly comfortable. The relaxation spreads deep in back of the throat, deep in back of the head and neck, deep into the neck and shoulders.

Let the arms relax. Relax the upper arms. Focus on the forearms and feel them relax. All the muscles between the elbows and wrists relax. The relaxation spreading across the tops of the hands and deep into the hands, deeply through the hands to the palms. Now the fingers relax all the way to the fingertips. As the fingers relax you may or may not experience a slight tingling in the fingers. If you do, you may find it to be a pleasing feeling.

Bring your attention back again to the relaxed muscles of the neck and shoulders. The relaxation flows into the chest and lungs. Your breathing is easy and gentle. You feel yourself relaxing more and more with each gentle breath.

You may relax more and more with each sound of my voice. All outside sounds are unimportant. Only the sound of my voice is important now.

Let the relaxation spread into the back. Feel it move gently down the back to the small of the back. Let all the muscles of the body go to sleep in a sense while you remain aware and focused. Feel the relaxation spreading around and deep into the sides of your torso. The muscles of the abdomen are relaxing deep into the abdomen.

As the muscles of the abdomen and hips relax, feel your subconscious open. This opening grows wider and wider. Accept my words into your mind. Gently conceive of the muscles in your belly and hips becoming firmer and firmer with a younger, leaner form and feel happy.

Now let the legs relax. The relaxation spreading into the thighs and knees. The calves of the legs relax, all the way to the ankles. In this relaxed state open your mind to conceive of how firm your legs are becoming.

Now let the feet relax—the heels of the feet, the soles of the feet, deep through the feet to the tops, and finally even the toes relax. It feels so good to relax and release all tension and care.

Enjoy a few moments of relaxation now as I slowly count from ten down to one. As I count, let your body relax more and more with each count. At the count of five, you may be more deeply relaxed than ever before. Then you may go even deeper as each number becomes smaller. Counting now: ten . . . nine . . . eight . . . seven . . . six . . . five . . . four . . . three . . . two . . . one . . . Rest.

Allow a wonderful peacefulness to surround your body as it becomes leaner and stronger. Feel good about this. Remember a favorite feeling and memory as your body effortlessly does the work.

As you drift and relax with your favorite feeling, your body can start becoming leaner, healthier, and stronger. Even as you soundly sleep, your body and mind are working on becoming leaner, healthier, and stronger. You will awaken in the morning feeling refreshed and ready for your day.

Play this tape nightly for three to eight weeks and then weekly for three months. Finally, play it once every three months for a year. Compare how far you progress from when you start to when you finish.

Gratitude—The Gift that Keeps on Giving

If you want to have more joy in your life, then look for joy in all things. If you want more grace in your life, surrender woe and be willing to look for grace. Granted, it's not always easy to do this. However, you can find the courage by rising to the challenge.

In the beginning it may be difficult to surrender an attitude of 'woe is me.' The key is to look for what's working in your life. This key is as simple as being thankful for even the smallest things every day.

Start small. Be grateful that you have a toothbrush and toothpaste. Make a list of everything for which you are grateful. Add to your list in incremental degrees every day.

Gratitude Technique

Write a letter to your Higher Power requesting, "Show me gratitude." Then go about your day, expecting insights about gratitude and being ready for them to surprise you. At the end of the day, write down in your journal what insights and experiences you received.

Gratitude Is Here and Now

Express gratitude for everything that is in your life today. On the most basic level, gratitude is simply accepting what is.

A woman named Janet wrote in her journal about all she had learned during the past month. She wrote of gratitude for her deepening ability to listen with her heart as she prayed to God. Once, as she was driving along Highway 95 on her way to work, she was reflecting on how thankful she was for her life. She noticed how her eating habits had been much more balanced recently. It seemed effortless because she was willing for it to be so. Her heart opened with joy and bliss.

She enjoyed this feeling of bliss for the rest of the half-hour drive. She said, "Even now I can feel the bliss in my heart in remembrance."

This was significant for Janet because she had struggled with hardship in her life in the past. For many years she asked, "Why? Why me? Why do I have so much trouble opening my heart?"

When she finally began to practice gratitude and did an exercise that taught her how to perceive from Soul (her true observant Self), she could see much more clearly than before. She saw without judgment that she had chosen to strengthen her emotional body through the experiences of this lifetime. Furthermore, as she released grief, fear, and rage, they were replaced by a feeling of expansiveness. She felt focused and connected to an open heart.

"Thank you," she whispered, realizing her Higher Power had been and always would be there to help her. "I am blessed," she wrote. "God's grace is with me." This was the gift that came with acceptance and being grateful.

The Three Rings of Forgiveness, Gratitude, and Grace

This technique involves gathering three rings that are meaningful to you. One ring symbolizes forgiveness, one ring symbolizes gratitude, and the third ring symbolizes grace.

Each morning hold these three rings and think of someone or something you love. Let the feeling of love fill and pour from your heart, encompassing the rings. As you place the rings on your fingers, say the following affirmations.

(1) Gratitude: "I am thankful for all the gifts in my life."

(2) Forgiveness: "I forgive myself and I forgive all life, fully and unconditionally."

(3) Grace: "I welcome joy into my mind, heart and body and lovingly accept all life."

Picture accepting your natural, healthy body image as you say these affirmations and put the rings on every morning and take them off every night. Wearing the rings daily can act as a reminder for you to practice the qualities of forgiveness, gratitude, and grace every day. Perform this ritual with the accompanying affirmations for three weeks to foster attitudes of forgiveness, gratitude, and grace.

The Gift of Grace

According to *Webster's Ninth Collegiate Dictionary,* grace relates to gratitude and goodwill. It is also a virtue coming from God, unmerited divine assistance, and a blessing that is an act of divine favor or compassion. Grace is an act of kindness or the quality of being considerate or thoughtful.

Grace can be passively accepted, but let's also look at it from an alternative, more active viewpoint, taking it one step beyond a passive state of waiting for divine intervention. Let's view grace as a quality that can be courted by taking action, and not expecting God to do for you what you can do for yourself. Courting grace gives Divine Spirit an active vortex through which to work.

Let's think of grace as being in accord with the ways of Divine Spirit. By doing so, we'd know how and when to behave in a more graceful manner, and when to act with forgiveness and gratitude. We'd know where, when and how to be more loving with ourselves and with others. By taking a dynamic role, we could become conduits for grace throughout the world.

Exploring the Parameters of Grace

To find out more about grace, answer the following questions in your journal. You can ask a trusted friend to help by reading the questions aloud to you. This way you can write down the first thing that pops into your mind. No second-guessing! The first thing that pops into your mind is your honest inclination.

(1) What does humility offer to help you understand grace?

(2) Who comes to mind when you think of the embodiment of humility and goodwill?

(3) How does this person show compassion for life?

(4) Does this person also illustrate self-realization and self-acceptance? How?

(5) How can you see yourself more honestly with compassion and love?

(6) How can you accept love for yourself as the initiation of receiving grace?

(7) How can you sustain the gift of grace on a daily basis? What can you do to further serve or realize this gift?

(8) What are you willing to do on a day-to-day basis to receive the grace that is always there for you because God loves you?

A Technique for Touching Grace

Stop and take several minutes to concentrate on grace. Close your eyes and imagine the feeling of grace. If it had a color, what would it be? What is the sound of grace? What is its scent? Does grace have a taste? How big is the grace that you are feeling? Can you compare it to something in the everyday world? Draw a picture that embodies the sight, sound, scent, taste, touch and feeling of grace.

Being More Open to Learning about Grace

How do you receive grace? In other words, the *process of receiving* is of foremost value and importance. How can you receive grace if you always give and never receive?

Let's imagine exploring a vast unknown vista with a flashlight, spotlighting one area at a time. Three elements I'd like to shine a light on will help you prepare to receive grace and understanding as love from your Higher Power.

The Flashlight Technique

(1) Ask to be open to receive an understanding about grace.
(2) Do your part by taking action. In other words, don't expect God to do for you what you won't do for yourself.
(3) Surrender the outcome to God, yet be ready to catch surprising insights moving into your life.

You can change the rate of your vibration using this flashlight technique. *Asking* opens you to the grace of Your Higher Power. *Doing* your part gives Spirit some action items with which to work. *Surrendering* the outcome is your way of allowing for God or Your Higher Power to work the outcome in the way, manner, order and time frame that's the best for all involved.

Many Sides of the Coin Called Grace

I need to practice all the subtleties of grace to really catch it. Part of the subtlety of grace is balance and acceptance.

Balance is integration of opposites or all things. The point of balance is at the center, where love is. When you catch true balance, your relationship with yourself changes. Your attitudes change as well as your beliefs about yourself and reality. You become equal to, instead of less than. The truth is that learning this state of balance deep in your heart is part of the price of earning freedom. To connect more deeply to the many-sided coin called grace, try incorporating the following three balances into your life starting today.

(1) Do something restful and calming that you enjoy every day.
(2) Do something kind for someone else each day, without letting anyone know about it.
(3) Say three times a day for the next four weeks, "I choose to be complete within myself and complete within my world."

Say this last affirmation until you believe it. Say it no matter what you may feel. Tape reminder cards on your bathroom mirror, computer, steering wheel, or whatever else is in your field of vision on a daily basis—anything to remind you to say it and believe it.

Control Panel Technique for Balance and Grace

Close your eyes. Look up at the imaginary spot in the center of your forehead where insight occurs in your brain. Conceive of yourself behind the wheel of the vehicle you most want in the world. A driving teacher sits next to you to help with the controls. You are now driving across a narrow floating bridge.

A half-circle gauge with the numbers one through twelve on its face dominates the control panel behind the wheel. See what number the red indicator arrow registers. Now ask the teacher to help you get the arrow to point to six in the center (your point of balance). Take your time doing this. When you feel completely balanced, thank the teacher for his or her help. Then open your eyes.

Take a drink of pure water to toast the health of your new body. Practice the control panel technique as often as you want so you can learn balance from the inside out. Balance is the key that opens the lock to the door of freedom.

When you accept and fully realize the attributes of forgiveness, gratitude and grace and make them your own, your heart will open wide like a river delta flowing to the sea. What an incredible feeling!

Attaining Freedom—-The Next Step on Your Journey

I know part of the reason you are reading this book is because you want to feel better while you balance your life and weight. But you'll find at this point in the journey that the adventure is just beginning on a much different level. In Chapter 10, discover how accepting self-responsibility and fostering self-love can empower you to cross the threshold to freedom.

Chapter 10
Self-Responsibility and Self-Love

Learning To Be Free—-The Next Step on Your Journey

By this time, you have progressed far in your journey toward weight balance. The following testimonials paint a picture of the before-and-after change of consciousness that occurs when you actively apply the principles outlined in this book. See if you can find the steps of realization, adjustment, and subsequent change to a higher level of consciousness in these stories of personal success.

"When I was in college, I dealt with the pressure of papers and exams by getting a pizza, a pint of chocolate ice cream, and a bag of cookies—eating them all and then writing or studying like a maniac all night.

"As a result, my weight constantly fluctuated. I'd put on ten or more pounds from bingeing, then starve myself to take it off fast, then put it on again. Thank goodness this pattern slowed down and took a turn for the better when I realized that pigging out wouldn't ease my real-world work stress. Once I admitted that binges didn't do much for me in my life now, they were easier to let go. I found other ways to relieve stress." –Jennifer, 30

"I used to have chocolate kisses on the counter, just to welcome customers. Candy wasn't my weakness, but pretty soon I became a social nibbler, grabbing a kiss with a customer every time we chatted about a printing job.

"I stopped doing this one day when a friend who was having problems with her husband came by four or five times to vent. By the end of the day, we had emptied the entire bowl of kisses.

"I went home that evening with a gross, sugar-and-fat feeling in my mouth and stomach. That gross sugar feeling woke me up to how much I ate while gabbing and made me think about all the food I unconsciously pop into my mouth at social gatherings (such as peanuts at bars and chips at parties). Through hypnosis I've made a point to be careful about what I pop into my mouth when I'm listening to others." –Heather, 26

"By the time I get home from work and all the stress there, it's 6:30 p.m. I'm exhausted and starving. I used to throw my stuff down and head to the kitchen, grabbing this and that—leftover noodles, cold cuts, bread—and eat as if I was inhaling them. But then one day, with a mouthful of granola, I thought, 'I don't want to eat this stuff. Why am I doing this?' I realized that frenzied snacking or shoveling it in was my way of releasing the stress of the day.

"Now I stay out of the kitchen until I calm down by using techniques that relieve my emotional stress. I take some time to figure out what I want to eat. That usually gets me eating healthier meals and has led to a better body weight." –Susan, 49

"My husband and I travel in our recreational vehicle while he writes books and consults with financial institutions. I don't particularly like accompanying him under these conditions. I realized that my resentments toward my husband were about giving up my previous way of life. Sacrificing everything to accommodate his second career caused me to feel rejected, angry, and hurt. It was only when I began to appreciate myself and renew my past interests that I found the metabolic menus started working—and my weight began to come off." – Fran, 60

"I learned to feel my anger by letting go of stubbornness. That was hard to do, but I did it. Before I'd just yell, hold on to the anger, and feel really guilty afterwards. Next I'd blame my parents or step-mom. Or I'd be sarcastic and make everything worse. When I stopped yelling and began talking about what was wrong, I found I felt better about me. That's when my eating balanced and I gave up purging." – Brittany, 16

"Every avenue I went down seemed blocked. All the people I knew were stuck in the past. I stayed home and ate out of loneliness.

"Then I learned to face my fear of people rejecting me. I practiced speaking up for my needs and wants. As I did this, I began to have more energy. I even tried new things, starting with having a cup of coffee at a Victorian tea room. Eventually, I began yoga class and dance lessons. My weight gradually slimmed down. I feel like a new person." – Mary, 72

Julie learned to love herself by taking time to make different, healthy food choices. Heather made unconscious snacking habits conscious in order to stop them. Jennifer dealt with stress realistically and found it easier to quit engaging in cycles of bingeing and dieting.

Fran reconnected with her true inner self and gracefully gave up resentments toward her husband. When she did, her weight balanced naturally. Brittany found inner coping skills that helped her process intense emotions. As a result, she balanced her weight *and* stopped her purging behavior.

Mary committed to face her fear of rejection, which led to having more fun in life as she became a slimmer woman of balance. These stories share real-life ways you too can overcome stumbling blocks that keep you from reaching your weight balance goals.

See How Far You've Come (What You've Achieved So Far)

I invite you to once again be aware of all the changes and the results, large and small, that you have attained so far. Feel good about your progress. By choosing to feel good about each change (and not wanting your whole body to transform magically in three weeks), you are on your way to a new body, a new state of consciousness, and loving it. I invite you to keep going for more. By reviewing your progress in this way, you'll be surprised to find your new body shifting each step along the way.

What the Techniques in This Chapter Will Do for You

The specific skill you'll glean from this chapter is a feeling of clarity in connection with your body image. The clearer you are, the more successful you'll become with manifesting your new body image. The insights you'll gain from this chapter will leave you feeling uplifted and calm. You'll be able to choose and manifest what you want in your life more each day.

Being in the Present Right Now

We all have ancestors. Last year's "you" could be your ancestor. However, because it is the past, it exists in memories. Only the present exists now. All else is irrational because the past does not exist for you now. Declare yourself alive and growing. Choose to be aware of endlessly giving birth to yourself in new and better ways.

An example of the need to continually expand into a newer state of being is illustrated in the following parable about seeing beyond your comfort zone. It is excerpted from Karen La Puma's book, *Awakening Female Power.*

Once upon a time, a frog lived in a deep well. She loved her home. It felt safe and secure and it was all she had ever known. She knew every corner, every crack, and every cranny of the well. One of her favorite things was to share what she knew about her well with others.

One day a sailor fetched water from the well. When he lowered the bucket, a curious thing jumped out and made a huge splash. With surprise, the well frog watched as the thing climbed onto the rock upon which she was sitting. It was another frog.

"Where did you come from?" asked the startled well frog.

"I came from a place far away, near a large body of water called the ocean."

"Oh! Is it this large?" the well frog asked, as she jumped to another rock across the well.

"No, it's really huge. Very big," answered the ocean frog.

The well frog thought *that* could not be true. That's wrong, she thought in total denial. She puffed herself up and used all her energy to jump from the rock all the way across to the wall of the well. With pride she announced, "Well, it can't be any bigger than this!"

The well frog limited her state of consciousness to what was known and familiar to her based on her past experience. She also got caught in the trap of vanity that her perspective about reality was *the* one-and-only right perspective.

Seeing from the Viewpoint of Soul

When we see with a more omniscient viewpoint (as the observer of life or Soul), then we see that the mind merely has likes and dislikes, without perceiving any "rights" or "wrongs" about a situation. A more Soul-oriented viewpoint can assist us in letting go of the past (even though it may be safe and familiar) to allow a larger and better view of what's possible to unfold before us.

Only by letting go of limiting past beliefs can we learn to discriminate and decide what is *best for the whole* in our purpose and goals. Holding the viewpoint of *what is best for the whole* helps us gain a larger awareness that *we* are part of a larger whole. Trusting this awareness allows us to begin to feel more complete within the entire universe and ourselves. Feeling complete also helps guide your actions effortlessly toward balancing your diet or eating style in a way that's naturally attuned to what's best for your whole body.

Learning Spiritual Intelligence

The key to weight balance depends on gaining a certain amount of spiritual intelligence that's based on how much control *you*, as Soul, have over your mind. When you learn and apply weight balance secrets for success, you're working with the Creative Force, which can be called your Higher Power, God, or any term you might use for the Divine.

Like the well frog, first we are trapped into believing our will or mind knows the only truth. Though we're secure in this knowledge, a much larger truth awaits discovery. The many techniques offered in this book give you the choice of experiencing a larger awareness in your quest for weight balance success. This larger awareness is balance.

You can choose to progress in spiritual intelligence by making a choice statement, such as, "I choose to be creative in reaching my goals." Then follow it with an appropriate action so your mind knows that you are serious.

Telling the Story of Your Life

What universal truth about human nature is presented here? The truth is this: The conscious and unconscious choices, and the ultimate actions you take based on them, results in telling the story of your life.

As this book revealed in Chapter 8 everything that's happening to you at this present moment is a result of choices (conscious as well as unconscious) made in the past. Every choice that you make *now* generates your future. Why not write your life story in your journal and discover ways you can begin to make more self-empowered choices for your health and new body, for yourself now and for future generations?

Self-responsibility Is the First Step to Grasping Change

One of the most crucial universal truths contained in this book is accepting responsibility. I know you've heard this with your ears and mind previously. Can you now hear this universal truth with your heart?

When we accept responsibility for the circumstances we face in the events that occur in our lives, *without blaming others or ourselves,* we change the perception of illusion in our lives forever. Taking responsibility is the first step to viewing all the "terrible situations" in life as opportunities to create something wonderful.

The More Self-Responsibility You Accept, the More Freedom You'll Have

Accepting self-responsibility is acknowledging and accepting truth for yourself. Acknowledging truth and freeing yourself from the quagmire of illusion is one way to show more love for yourself.

Do you remember how it felt to be caught in illusion? Remember believing that you had to be this size or that? Remember the limitations on your life when you perceived that doing something for yourself meant depriving or hurting someone else? Remember how self-defeating and constraining the illusion of "dieting will work this time" was? As you know, these illusions are hypnotic traps of preoccupation for the mind and ego. Choosing a persistent path *away* from illusion can lead you toward more success and more open doorways to weight balance.

> *Illusion-Busting Technique*
> *(1) Close your eyes and look upward at the insight area of your brain while connecting to your Higher Power. Imagine your Higher Power in front of you.*
> *(2) Chant a word that means love while asking to perceive an insight that is true and helpful to your unfoldment as Soul right now. Do this for about five to ten minutes, then fall into silent contemplation.*
> *(3) Listen for an answer from your Higher Power. When you are ready, open your eyes and write down what you perceived.*

A Tale of Self-responsibility in Action

A patient named Michelle felt stagnant in her life. She had trouble applying all she had learned about empowering herself toward improving her life. She was on the verge of making a major decision about marrying the man she had been dating for the past two years.

After seven weeks of gathering information and having experiences that showed her what she needed to know to make the decision, I asked, "What do you feel in your gut?"

"I'm not happy in this relationship," she said.

"What do you want to do about it?" I asked.

"I want to avoid facing this and talking to him. Yet, I know talking to him is what I most need to do," she admitted.

"How is this the best course of action for you?"

"If I keep avoiding, it will eat at me. I'll end up compulsively eating just to numb out and make my mind be still," she explained.

"What could you do about that?"

"Face it and get it over with," she said firmly. "I will talk to him soon."

Michelle knew that it was time to move on from the relationship. She took responsibility for herself and her actions to get what she wanted from the relationship, not settling for less. She used patience up to this point in time, allowing the situation to show her if this was truly what she wanted in a relationship. Michelle realized she could not change her boyfriend—she could only take responsibility for herself.

Michelle discovered that she felt burdened in her thoughts and emotions. She was stuck in her own past pattern of fearing guilt about hurting someone else's feelings. She became a victim of her own fears.

Michelle realized that surrendering her fears of feeling guilty and choosing to be assured in her own self-esteem would allow new opportunities to happen for herself and her soon-to-be ex-boyfriend.

The opposite of the "poor me, victim consciousness" is taking action and responsibility for what you want in life. The choice is to turn the situation into an opportunity to grow and learn or wallow in a victim consciousness.

Did Michelle take the responsibility and stand up for her truth? Yes, she did; and because she resolved the underlying conflict within herself, her self-esteem was boosted as well as her motivation to keep her food intake balanced.

Like a River Flowing Freely to the Sea

The following four steps will help you with the challenge to accept more self-responsibility for your life.

(1) Begin by simply writing the following statement in your journal fifteen times daily until it happens: "Please, Higher Power show me how to accept responsibility. Thank you."

(2) Be aware that answers can come in many ways. Journal about them when they appear in contemplation or your daily life.

(3) Contemplate the answers. Journal the highest spiritual insights from your contemplations.

(4) Repeat these three steps as often as necessary, until you attain results. Remember, accepting self-responsibility is one way to love yourself more.

Planting Seeds of Love and Acceptance

This one is simple since the previous techniques have prepared the ground. Now is the time to plant seeds as you persevere and trust your process. The following fable illustrates how a lack of perseverance with patience can be a downfall.

A farmer was too eager for harvest and wanted to help his crops grow. In the middle of the night he went outside and pulled on the new shoots, compromising the health of his crop. In other words, he tried to "push the river."

This attitude of trying to push the river is as error-ridden as trying to hurry a harvest and trying to rush to your goals. You can't hasten the goal of shaping your body. Everything happens in good time, so connect with patience. Be aware your own process has its own season and flow, which can lead to harvesting self-esteem and acceptance of your body image.

Plant seeds by writing the following positive statement fifteen times a day for four weeks: "I love and approve of myself." New sprouts of inner self-esteem link to higher consciousness. With a higher state of awareness comes a degree of perception and clarity beyond description.

Freedom from Illusion

A woman named Rebecca has two sisters. One sister is older than Rebecca and one is younger. Both sisters are large women. Rebecca says, "Even my aunts and grandmother are large women. I'm the only one in my family who is tiny."

Rebecca never talks about her weight because it isn't a problem to her. She feels there are other areas of her life that need attention, such as stress at work or stress with her spouse.

You might think that Rebecca is tiny because of what she says and believes. She has no anguish about her size or weight. In fact, she also says that her breasts are perfect. Rebecca is a size fourteen.

Rebecca is free in this area of her life—free of the illusion that she has to worry about her weight. She is free to be who she is, free to be happy with herself.

Reconciling the Conflicting Images of Woman

The book *Return of the Great Goddess* edited by Burleigh Muten scans the past hundred years for the archeological discoveries of more than one thousand artifacts of female icons. These icons, dating from circa 30,000 to 9000 B.C., confirm the sociological relevance of the Great Goddess. For twenty thousand years, the Great Goddess was acknowledged in myth and revered in religious imagination. The results of many archeological digs found coal, bone, and stone females with great egg-shaped bellies, breasts, and buttocks. All showed the fullness of the creative impulse as manifested in the human female form.

It is an art to develop healthy self-esteem in today's world of denigration of the normal feminine form. Each person on an individualized level can resolve these social prejudices.

When you choose to resolve the constraining social roles about women, you learn to let go of the staid, conventional, socially limiting restrictions of what-it-is-to-be-a-woman. You then enter the unknown—an often misunderstood, scary time. Yet, the unknown can be a time of great discovery and personal affirmation an exciting, dynamic time when you never felt so fully alive.

Visit a Museum Technique

The introverted fear of female fat creeps along, infiltrating our culture in as much the same way as a cold war or hate campaign might. This cultural brainwashing can easily get mistranslated into hate against our female bodies. By merely exposing ourselves to cultural beliefs, often we unknowingly allow more of the prejudices (than we'd like to accept) to interject themselves into our psyches and ultimately the fabric of our lives.

My purpose here is to open up different, wider viewpoints so that you can be more aware of how you might respond alternatively when you let go of reacting subconsciously to the beauty myths in culture today.

I began a quest to find full-figured models in history to counter the petite myth and bought a book called *Myths of Greece and Rome*, by Bryan Holme. I was fascinated by the illustrations, many of which portrayed the female form in lush flesh and soft, flowing lines. One called "Leda and the Swan" by Leonardo da Vinci shows the fullness of the female body in all its beauty as Leda caresses the swan. These pictures soothe my eyes into accepting a more alluring, voluptuous female form.

A feeling of peacefulness envelops me while I view this picture. I feel completeness as I view the true spirit of womanhood embodied in flesh. How refreshing.

Check out any similar book from the library or visit a museum where paintings of the Old Masters are shown. Even good prints of their work will do to help you reestablish a healthy regard for the feminine form (like Rebecca has).

You, too, can develop a healthy self-esteem, free from the constraints of the pressures of our culture. Freeing yourself from false images ultimately leads to the path of empowerment.

What Is Empowerment?

The view of empowerment according to Hippocrates, the father of medicine, is that nothing else produces joys, delights, laughter, grief, and despondency but the brain. Yet in Persian culture, the legendary Persian physician Avicenna (A.D. 980-1037) said the imagination not only acts on one's own body but also other's bodies at great distances. (Persian philosophy believes that thoughts are real and can reach out to influence realms beyond this one.)

I say take the best of both worlds—use your mind *and* imagination to influence your reality and change your world. Empowerment begins with cutting through the illusions. Yet, most of us need structure and form. You may have been out of control with your eating in the past. Or you may have been so in control that you were overly controlling of everything. Either scenario is out of balance with the natural flow of the universe. Empowerment is finding what balance means in your life by taking responsibility for your own thoughts, feelings, and actions.

Tools to Help You Empower Yourself

The following technique will help increase your self-esteem and love for your true Self (as in self-caring, not selfish). When you love yourself, then you can truly give to others from the space of an open heart. Holding an open heart with higher consciousness leads to weight balance success.

Empowerment Technique

(1) Close your eyes and look upward to the insight area of your brain. Conceive of a beautiful sound and then a favorite color.

(2) Gently remember a time when you had an experience of valuing what was inside of you as true riches. Be aware that your heart is open now. How is this for you? How do you feel when your heart is open? Write this down in your journal.

Truth is freedom. When you choose to accept truth as what is and start taking steps toward where you want to go, you will achieve success. Be present, sincere, and trust your process.

Centering with Beauty and Stillness

We, as women, dream and walk our path of fullness and beauty. I have found that many spiritual answers, such as how to center and find stillness, are found by being aware of practical, down-to-earth matters.

You may think of traveling far in order to meet a diet guru and receive enlightenment. Yet the temple of true knowledge is within. Remember, nothing outside of you gives freedom. Only the journey within nourishes freedom. The following parable illustrates this principle of valuing the journey within.

> *In ancient times, at the beginning of the cosmos and the universes, God decided that Soul was so precious It needed to be hidden somewhere safe. So God hid It in the heart of all humans because no one would think to look for it there.*

The operative word here is "think." Intellectualizing removes you from the heart center. Centering in the beauty of the heart is where all true motivation exists.

Breathing Free as a New Baby's Breath

Through active participation, learn how your breath can help you get a second wind, gain motivation, or renew your purpose. Try this from the unique point of view of recognizing yourself as the spiritual being that you are. As a spiritual being, you have one experience after another. All you need to do is take one step deeper into your experiences, let go of old feelings and thoughts, and be aware. You were born with the ability to use your energies in free-flowing ways. You were born to breathe freely, enjoy life and make the most of it.

A Breathing Exercise for Feeling Free

Wherever you are, whenever you feel tense all over, close your eyes and imagine your favorite place on earth. As you inhale, see this safe place. And you exhale, see yourself completely relaxed in this place. Smell the air. Hear the sounds around you. Reach out and touch something near you and describe the feeling to yourself.

Let the air breathe you as you feel your breath enter your nose, flow down your windpipe and into your belly. Let your belly expand with the energy of your breath. Feel this life process as a mystery that renews you constantly without effort. Simply be aware of your breath. To relax and touch base with feeling free, practice this technique at least once a day.

Making Freedom Happen by (Fill-in-the-Blank) Technique

In the following exercise, just let the first thing you think of pop into your mind. No second-guessing! Then write your answers to the questions in your journal. This exercise can also be shared and done with a close friend. Prepare to be surprised by the wisdom that's revealed.

(1) Remember the most favorite activity you ever experienced. Close your eyes for a minute and recall the episode and expect perfect memory. Let the images and sensations associated with this experience flow into your mind. Describe the event by writing down the details, beginning with the words, "I was . . ."

(2) Gently remember the most loving feelings you ever experienced. Close your eyes and allow the memory to come to mind. It might have revolved around someone you loved, a beloved pet, or an activity? Close your eyes and remember what your heart felt like when you loved. After opening your eyes, describe how it was for you in writing, starting with the words, "I remember loving . . ."

(3) Close your eyes and remember joyfully and successfully accomplishing something after a time of learning and practicing. Write about what you

accomplished and the feelings that accompanied your success. Begin with "I accomplished . . ." or "When I accomplished _____, I felt . . . I heard . . . I remember seeing . . ."

(4) Remember a time when you were in trouble. How did you figure a way out of it? Remember other ways you may have used your creative power to get free of trouble at other times in your life. Write about your memories.

What unique outlook helped you overcome adversity? What did you say and do? You can use this memory exercise anytime you need to tap your creative depths and become more free from the troubles you perceive are binding you.

The Choice of Where to Go Is Always Determined by You

Many techniques in this book give you ways to strengthen yourself to meet the challenges of life and the situations in which you find yourself now. These techniques can help you choose new and different ways to reach and sustain your peak, bringing good health, weight balance success, happiness, and prosperity into your life—or not. It's your choice. It's a matter of understanding where you are now and choosing to move beyond the present by placing your attention and focusing your efforts on where you want to be.

Understanding the Mystery and Paradigm of Cycles

Knowing how cycles work in your life is a precious pearl of truth. Like the pearl, it's also a symbol of the deep mysteries of life. You can learn a great deal by studying the cycles of nature that affect individuals, family units, nation groups, and races.

The fluctuating cycles of human life work within the parameters of universal laws. The cycles of birth and death, day and night, sleeping and waking, the four seasons of the year, the four periods of human drama (birth, growth, youth, and old age) are some of the most common human cycles.

Human life cycles can be diminished through ignorance of the universal laws. For example, longevity can be destroyed through vice and debauchery, leading to a downgraded state of health and diminished success in life. Anyone who is low in mental or physical health is at greater risk to succumbing to vice, a complication of the downward spiral.

Successfully rejuvenating the body and living healthily to an advanced age relies on proper nutrition (sometimes by supplementing with a regimen of vitamins and minerals), proper exercise, and good self-esteem. If you alter your diet or activity level, your aging process will change along with your weight balance.

By halting or reversing the aging of glands (especially the pituitary gland), you'll begin to feel your cycles changing toward youth again.

To have youth and weight balance success, you must have empowerment and imagination, using both to secure a place in this world. It's all a matter of being clear on what direction you choose and focusing your attention and efforts on which way you want to go.

Understanding Your Personal Cycles Technique

Try the following exercise to better *Understand Your Personal Cycles.* Answer all the questions, then ask, "How can I understand the cycle I am in right now? What could strengthen my awareness and help me choose to ascend, wherever I am in my cycle?"

Understanding Your Personal Cycles

(1) *Follow the timeline and mark a red "X" on where you are now.*
Birth and Growth
    1-2-3-4-5-6
        7-8-9-10-11-12
            13-14-15-16-17-18
                19-20-21-22-23-24 (4 cycles of 6 years each)

Youth

    25-26-27-28-29-30
        31-32-33-34-35-36
            37-38-39-40-41-42
                43-44-45-46-47-48
                    49-50-51-52-53-54
                        55-56-57-58-59-60 (6 cycles of 6 years each)

Old Age
61-62-63-64-65-66
    67-68-69-70-71-72
        73-74-75-76-77-78
            79-80-81-82-83-84
                85-86-87-88-89-90
                    91-92-93-94-95-96 (6 cycles, 6 years each)

(2) *Now write a list of significant life events in your journal. Be sure to write the date and how old you were at the time.*

(3) *Take a yellow highlighting pen and put an "X" on the timeline where a significant event occurred, such as getting married, the birth of a child, deaths, graduations, a residential move, and different diets. Notice the cycles. Mark the major turning points in your life. Ask yourself about your possible life patterns. Do you see a pattern of two-, three-, four-, six-, or twelve-year cycles? This doesn't have to be exact, just approximate. Trust what you see as your cycle of change.*

(4) *Ask God or Your Higher Power for insight and wisdom on what there is for you to learn about your cycles.*

(5) *Take notes about the insights you receive. There's no right or wrong way to do this exercise.*

Now that you know where you are in your cycles, you can see that taking one step at a time—starting now—can bring you to the top of this cycle in the best health and weight balance. Start good habits now and you can build them into the cycles that follow as shown in the above timeline.

Knowledge of cycles can help with your awareness of life and nutrition, keeping you growing on the positive side of the loop. All this renews body, mind, and spirit for a longer, happier, more fulfilled life.

What Is Diet Success?

My answer to this question comes from more than forty-three years of struggling with disordered eating and over seventeen years of clinical work with others *plus* fifteen years of counseling in choosing nutritionally dense foods for excellent health.

> *Diet success is a choice you make daily by being willing to keep taking the steps outlined in this book. Releasing doubts, anger, cynicism, and hostility for the personal experience of what it truly means to be free insures that you'll never be the same again.*

Through reading this book, you've found ways to continually love, encourage, and trust yourself on the path of a healthy eating style. Practicing these principles daily is a habit, a discipline, but above all else, an art form.

Life beyond Diet Success

This book has given you a taste of how much more life has to offer through its keys to accessing the wealth of your experiences. Maybe you've glimpsed insights and a vision of the personal freedom that can be yours if you continue to evolve in consciousness by (1) asking questions, (2) taking steps forward after receiving the answers, and (3) finding support systems that continue to help you evolve even more.

The Cornerstone in the Foundation of Your Success

I believe trust in yourself is *the* major cornerstone in the foundation of your success. With honesty and trust, you can continue your process of unfoldment, gaining greater spiritual insights and new revelations as discoveries on this journey of life reveal the richness of you. For more on the journey of discovery that waits beyond maintaining the new you, turn to Chapter 11.

Chapter 11
The Journey Beyond...

Living a Life of Health, Balance, and Freedom—Now and in the Future

Can you connect with the present-day feeling that there's more to life? From your experiences throughout this book, I hope you've not only seen but also proven to yourself that there's much more than you previously expected.

Think about your state of mind at the beginning of this book. At that time you might have connected with the concept that life isn't giving you enough. In your quest to get enough, you may have struggled for more control over food through dieting, bingeing, or purging. Or you might have indulged in excessive shopping or overconsumption in any form. These are natural recourses to turn to (and act out) in an effort to fill the void we perceive in our lives.

When you choose to poke the spiritual fire within (as you have done by reading and practicing the techniques throughout this book), you always gain much more—more health and more freedom to be who you've always wanted to be.

Keys for Maintaining the New You

The keys for maintaining the new you are more attitudinal than anything else. First and foremost, know that you are a shining essence of Divine Spirit—Soul.

Souls who shine brightest find ways to give back to the world from the essence of their new selves through their work and creatively through what they have to offer the world. Once you've incorporated what you've received from Divine Spirit, the natural course of an aware Soul is to serve others. The ways in which you choose to serve the world through your work and your creativity also help you grow further in mastery of the principles found in this book.

The Six Steps of Mastery for Making Your Dreams Come True

Your strength as Soul is awesome, considering you use the creativity, potential, and mastery of Soul and the Holy Spirit to realize and live your dreams. What are the six steps to mastery? Let's review the reciprocal relationship that occurs between you and Divine Spirit when you decide to transform your life and manifest your dreams.

The first thing is to (1) *ask* for what you want to receive. Divine Spirit then opens opportunities so that (2) you can *take action*. Taking action is *the* sign Spirit needs before giving you more opportunities, and (3) a *grateful heart* keeps you open to receive more. When Spirit gives you even more, it's time for (4) *imagining* even more of your dream and (5) *surrendering* the outcome to Spirit by allowing It to work on Its timetable. Last comes (6) time to *rest and review* through contemplation. Remember to be grateful by thanking your Higher Power, Divine Spirit, and God daily (blessings flow more easily to a grateful heart). Then you (with the assistance of your Higher Power) can start the cycle all over again.

The rest of this chapter is devoted to exploring what it takes to live your dreams. Let's begin by checking in with your purpose statement and your present state of being. The power to experience and manifest your dreams is not in yesterday or tomorrow, but only in today because Soul lives in the present moment.

Checking In with Your Current Purpose Statement Technique

Please restate your current purpose statement.
My purpose is _____.

Has your purpose statement changed since the beginning of the book? What part of it changed? Maybe your purpose statement changed many times throughout this book. The changes may be subtle or conspicuous.

Regarding the subtle changes: What can you do to honor the shifts of awareness that you have experienced already? The subtlest changes are the ones that best help you maintain your balance so moving forward becomes effortless. The knowing, aware Soul learns to pause, acknowledge, and value these changes. Pat yourself on the back if you picked out subtle changes in your progress and purpose statement. Chronicle these changes in your journal.

If you can't find subtle or obvious changes, please take heart. Often the harder we try at something, the worse it gets. Actually trying too hard can reverse your effort with a pile-up of forced energy, like a car pile-up on a major highway. Be willing to let go and flow into what's next for your purpose. Expending the effort to do this is ultimately worth it. We'll explore how to fine-tune a future purpose statement later in this chapter.

Visualization: Fuel for Your Body in Your New Future

Hold on to your seats; this is your captain speaking. We're going for the ride of our lives. We are now landing in a country unlike any you've ever known. Some things may appear familiar, yet be prepared for the unusual. The natives are friendly, gentle, and calm with an imperceptible glow about them that you will love and want to make your own.

As you step off the plane, walk down a plush carpet thick with rose petals strewn by our native hosts. The perfume of the flowers is aromatic. Imagine a tall blonde woman or a man with curly, brown hair approaches and offers you a soma drink. Your escort then leads you to a private patio where others are seated at round tables, talking and laughing together.

As you sip your drink, it gently wipes out all memory of processed foods of any kind. You lean over to ask other guests, "Have you ever tasted or experienced anything like this before?"

"No," they answer. You'd like to have a private supply of this in your home.

Soft flute music wafts through the air as the musicians arrive. They manifest as beings of shimmering light. Their faces glow with great light while you're in their presence. Listening to the flute feels so light and blissful. It's like no other feeling you've ever had. In fact, you want this feeling to last forever.

As you continue sipping the soma drink, you feel the wind caress your arms and face like the stroking of a thousand velvet fingertips. Your escort invites several others to join you for dinner. The menu is illuminated under the glass tabletop. It's made of a filmy airy material that changes as you read it. The waiter explains that the menu responds to your brain waves. It is activated by and aligned to your individual body chemistry via sensors in your chair. The dishes are named to excite you, as if your body, mind, and spirit are responding in a symphony of harmony.

You glance at the others and smile, wondering, what could this lead to in my life? An answer will come. You know the answer will come to you—either in your dreams or waking dreams.

Using Dream Time for Your Future Endeavors

Throughout this book I've used stories from dreams and other sources to help prompt you to gain awareness and a sense of adventure. Dream time can become a part of your life that is effortless. You can use it to get answers about everything from what foods are right for your body today to what course of action is best for your life tomorrow.

When I first started writing my dreams, I was hostile and often frustrated. I wanted answers *right now*. Yet for years the answers eluded me. All the while I had many exciting times in my dreams.

Some people might look at these exciting dreams as nightmares, but now I see them as challenges that filled my life with mysteries waiting to be solved. It took a few years of working with dreams and the assistance of my Higher Power before they began to take on an adventurous quality though. By choosing to see my dream experiences in this way, I learned how to ask good questions to get answers about my future. Sound easy? It is. Here's how.

Mocking Up Desire for Dreams of the Future

The first thing you need is desire. Mock up a strong desire.

If you can't do that, then remember a time when you felt excited. Get into that exciting memory and let it just pop into your mind. Re-live the memory as best you can. Be there now. Describe it to yourself out loud in a little story. Get into the feelings and fully experience the excitement surrounding that memory.

Ask yourself, "Where do I feel this excitement in my body?" No second-guessing! Let the first thing pop into your mind.

Then ask, "What color is this excitement? What shape is this excitement?" Let the answers pop into your mind, even if they don't make sense. Do it even though you might feel silly. These feelings are okay. Go through them and go with them.

If you still feel a part of yourself wants you to stop, see it for what it is. That judging part of you will usually find fault with everything. If you find yourself thinking, "Oh, that's not going to work," then stop and take a few deep breaths. Ask your Higher Power to help you adjust the negative reaction right now.

Then take this tangible memory of excitement and say out loud "I want to remember my dreams of the future." Say it with passion and write it in your journal. Keep your journal by your bed and use it to record what you dream.

The Prime Obstacle to Recording Your Dreams

If you say, "Oh, I'll write it down later," you'll discover that the dream often disappears when you're ready to record it. As soon as you make a new habit (such as writing down your future dreams), remember to mock up desire for the results that you seek. As the new behavior becomes automatic, you'll continue to follow through with it. The more you practice it, the easier it becomes until it is as automatic as breathing. Then the subconscious takes over with little effort.

> *Remember, if you think you can, you can! If you think you can't, you can't. Either way you are right. That's the power of the mind.*

Choose to train your mind to think you *can* and it will happen.

Keys to Using Dream Time for Your Future Advantage

Use your dream time for your future advantage by *first* training yourself to effortlessly remember your dreams. *Second,* learn to record your dreams when you first become conscious, upon awakening each morning. *Third,* after several weeks begin to write questions you want answered in your dream journal. This works best if you ask one question at a time and wait for as long as it takes to receive the answer.

Asking too many questions at once can overwhelm you and lead to confusing insights. Feel free to keep asking the same question for weeks. I often ask a question for months because some core questions need that much time to reveal their answers to you. Other insights may come within a few days. I choose to be surprised and amused by the process, instead of trying to dictate or control it in any way.

The Wisdom of Your Inner Voice Found in Dreams

Use the above "dream time asking technique" to find what foods are good for your body. Or alter the questions to find out answers about your future and your life (as I did in the questions that follow in the parentheses). Expect to be surprised by the answers!

(1) What foods do I need to eat today? (What direction do I need to go with my life?)

(2) What is best for my body? (What is best for my future?)

(3) Show me what to add to my food plan. (Show me what priorities to add to my life.)

(4) What food can I learn to let go of eating? (Which activities can I release or say "no" to?)

(5) Show me what to do for balanced eating. (Show me what to do for a future of health, freedom, and love.)

Feel free to ask to be shown more than you need to know. Be sure to thank your Higher Power for helping you with these insights.

Keys to Discovering and Understanding Your Small Inner Voice

Prepare yourself to be open to the prompting of Divine Spirit through your small inner voice by exploring the following questions.

Write down the answers to these questions in your journal after contemplating upon them with your Higher Power.

(1) What abilities do I need to develop to understand my inner voice?

(2) What new strength do I want to take form that I can apply to understanding my small inner voice?

Consciously Listening to Your Inner Voice to Find the Next Step

One way to learn to listen to your inner voice is to journal both your waking dreams and sleeping ones. Jot down clues or symbols as they appear in your dreams or life each day.

When I wrote the first question from the above exercise in my journal, I woke up the next morning and heard my inner voice say, "Explore the love of learning."

I was tempted to minimize what I heard by simply forgetting. My actions clearly illustrated that in my grogginess (that state between waking and sleeping) I was beginning to forget how precious the gift of awareness is. I almost seemed willing to compromise my quest for inner truth for the habit of mental laziness.

Instead, I chose to combat the laziness I felt. I asked, "What new strength do I want to take form as I explore the love of learning?"

I decided one way to get the answer to this question on a cellular level was by writing a core statement fifteen times every day. I wrote it until it eventually manifested in my life. It turned out to be an effective exercise for me to overcome a lazy brain. The statement I wrote fifteen times a day that I needed to know with my whole heart was *I am appreciated.*

Further into the process I asked in my journal, "What value can I receive from this experience?" My small inner voice whispered, "Freedom."

Freedom implies full knowledge of you. Freedom, like love, can not be erased. Both are states of higher consciousness. Moments of giving and receiving love, like freedom, live in your heart forever.

Warnings from Your Small Inner Voice

Your small inner voice may remind or warn you about ways the negative habits of the mind will try to trip you on your journey to greater awareness, as my mind attempted to do in the above example.

Instead of becoming caught up in a *feedback loop* of blame, shame or retribution against yourself, choose to value what you've learned from the experience. Let go of any self-punishing thoughts or emotions that revolve around your initial reactions to the challenges that face you. When you find yourself starting to spin into a feedback loop, write answers to the following questions in your journal.

(1) What emotions have I navigated so far?
(2) What feelings am I willing to take charge of?
(3) How will I do it and continue to accept the keys of freedom (from my Higher Power and my small inner voice) as they are given to me?

Keeping Your Connection Open

Throughout this book, I asked you to interact with the material by engaging in writing techniques, visualizations and exercises. From the process of reading and experiencing this book, you've grown strong and flexible—emotionally, physically and mentally. This chapter explores what it means to develop that same level of strength and flexibility spiritually, in preparation of your next adventure.

To keep your spiritual connection open, try practicing the techniques given in this chapter for five, ten, or twenty minutes a day. It's easy and brief. You may not be aware of changes right away, but that's not important. What *is* important is to trust and keep your connection to Divine Spirit open, to become stronger spiritually by developing "spiritual muscle" in as much the same way that you develop physical muscle to stay fit.

The Spiritual Quality of Doing without Doing

Have you ever found yourself engaged in a long involved process for work? Many times we daydream as we work by routine or habit and enter into another state of consciousness. Could you remember every part of the task? No. You put your body in motion and then daydreamed while you did it.

Could you remember all the motions you did? No. Entering this zone of "doing without concentrating on what you're doing" is an altered state of consciousness. What's important is that the job was completed. You did it well and didn't have to remember every detail every step of the way. Contemplate upon the concept of doing without doing. Ask to understand its true spiritual significance. Journal the insights that you receive.

Learning by Doing It for Yourself

Have you ever had the experience of wanting to learn how to do an activity and feeling frustrated when someone else tried to do it for you?

I once asked a friend to help me learn to use a newsletter computer program. I was excited and eager to learn and I had some basic MacWrite experience. He sat down in front of his computer and I sat to his right, watching as he showed me how to do it.

As he gave me one term after another to remember, I began to feel frustrated and fearful that I'd never retain it all. My body slumped and I felt my mind wanting to drift off in a daydream. This can happen to anyone who's trying to learn something new when they're *just* not getting it.

I stopped him, leaned back, took a deep breath, and said, "I need to actually do this myself. Could I sit where you're sitting and do it while you explain it to me?" That one action changed everything. When I touched the keyboard, looked at the monitor screen and became actively involved with the material, I started to get it.

If I hadn't known to check with my small inner voice for that intuitive flash of insight, I'd have given up. I probably would have had a less-than-rewarding experience trying to make a newsletter. Yet I learned and mastered the skills to operate a computer and the software by listening inwardly, getting a subtle nudge to move in a certain direction, and then acting upon it with a sense of mastery.

Life is structured in this way. You might start by reading this book, seeing your life reflected in its examples. Yet soon you're ready to interact and get hands-on experience through the techniques, visualizations, and exercises. This is *the way* of learning by doing.

As you learn to appreciate and regularly contact your spiritual intuition (your small inner voice), the more aware you'll become. Eventually it will become effortless and natural for you to recognize and take the next step on your journey of freedom.

Let go of things that impede your progress and direct your attention toward that which assists you. It will make your life more balanced and bring more joy and ease to every day.

Being Practical

One of my patients was blocked and struggling with the issue of taking the next step toward being responsible for keeping herself balanced in all areas of her life.

"I just can't seem to get this," she said.

Finally I asked her to close her eyes, relax and breathe. "Place you inner attention on the center of your forehead where insight occurs in your brain. Now connect with your Higher Power as you know it. Say inwardly, 'Higher Power, I surrender this problem.' Now imagine a beautiful sound, a loving feeling, and a favorite color."

She did this for several minutes. When she opened her eyes, the struggle was gone and she felt better, more open to taking her next step.

Later on I shared this story with a colleague. I asked, "Why did it take me so long to put my attention on my Higher Power, which prompted me to remind my patient to reconnect with her Higher Power and surrender the situation?"

My colleague didn't have an answer, but she smiled. She understood how we sometimes forget to put our attention on our Higher Power when we feel blocked or are struggling with an issue, situation, attitude, or belief.

She related that once she worked with a client who came to the first session in a panic and who paced the office the entire time she talked. Soon my colleague remembered an exercise for the patient to try to connect with her Higher Power. This one involved closing her eyes and singing the word "HU" softly (pronounced like the word *hue*).

Spirit, your Higher Power, and God will work in your life—at the office, at home, anywhere. You will receive the protection and comfort you need if you remember to stay connected to your spiritual resources. *Remembering* is the key—the sooner, the better.

> *"HU is an ancient name for God,"*

She explained. "Sing it in a long, drawn-out way, like this," she suggested. "HU-U-U-U-U." Within a few moments, the client calmed down enough to sit while she conversed.

Take Time to Rest and Review

Sometimes we're in a hurry to get on with life. When I read a book, I often plunge through it like a thirsty traveler in a desert with no water for five miles. For five metaphorical miles, I'll push myself to get to the water at the next oasis—push myself to read as fast as I can to see what's next.

I do this in life too, pushing myself to finish one project so I can move on to the next one. When is it the time to relax and enjoy the present moment? The answer to this question is why I created the *Rest and Review Celebration* technique.

Reviewing how far you've come is a way to validate and honor your process. A time of rest, review, and celebration invites the honored guest of insight. When the guest of honor finally arrives, you'll find that it is *you!* Later you will honor the gifts you have received on your quest.

One Way to Do the Rest and Review Celebration Technique

Think of each step that you've taken along the way like a dear friend you haven't talked to in a month. It's time to reconnect. In other words, it's time to invite, acknowledge, and treat every step you've taken in this process as the honored guests that they are.

Make an "honored guest list" of your steps so far in your journey of balanced eating. List them all, big or small, grand or minute, flashy or not. All are important—be sure to slight none of them.

How do you prepare? Decide on a date and time. Since this is a rest and review, maybe you'll wear lounging clothes to your celebration. Set the scene in a unique way that makes it special for you. Maybe you'll light scented candles.

This *Rest and Review Celebration* is one way to crisply delineate and put closure on the completion of this cycle.

When you started reading this book, you met the antithesis of its principles when you faced problems and obstacles along the way. When you used the techniques in the book, you grew and transformed to become even greater than you ever imagined you'd be.

Now we're at the final step: synthesis. Synthesis is pulling together all the steps you've taken and reflecting on what you've learned. Synthesis happens most naturally when you take time to do the following technique.

Visualize arriving at your celebration and turning on the lights. As you enter the space devoted to the celebration, be aware of the moment when you light the room (or light your scented candles). As light fills the room, capture the moment in your memory by putting your attention upon it. Ask yourself to be aware of catching insights as you turn the light on each step you've taken in your journey throughout this book.

Take time to welcome and acknowledge everyone on your "honored guest list." As you review the chronology of steps you've taken in your journey of balanced eating, take time to feel gratitude for the hidden gifts each step has brought to you. Recognize how the steps took you beyond your problems and stretched you into a greater awareness. Chronicle your realizations and gratitude in your journal.

Now it's time to celebrate. Close your eyes and write down the biggest three things you've learned from your journey—those things you're most grateful for having learned. Take time to reflect as you rest. Close your celebration by singing HU with gratitude and a few moments of quiet reflection.

Resting and reviewing is a way to renew you. Soon enough, more challenges will enter your life. Prepare yourself to stay open so that the spiritual awareness and creativity from Divine Spirit keeps coming.

Contemplation

Daily contemplation is a form of renewal, a mini-time of rest and review. The contemplative techniques in this book can be adapted to fit your ever-changing needs. Choose one time of each day to devote to a daily contemplation period so you can sustain the results of your spiritual intuition.

Each contemplation period starts with closing your eyes. Then look upward to the center of your forehead as you connect with your Higher Power. You may have a favorite sound or word you can chant or sing for five to ten minutes. Then fall into silence for a few more minutes and enjoy the peace.

If thoughts interrupt you during this peaceful quiet time, focus on a natural sound within earshot for a few minutes. Since all sounds are of God, enjoy the sound as you release whatever is bothering you. Allow bothersome thoughts to glide on the air currents and dissipate as if they were as insubstantial as clouds.

Contemplate on the Delights of Success

Close your eyes and focus your attention upward to the center of your forehead. Take a minute to contemplate upon the delights of the weight balance success you've attained, now living beyond the reach of the coercive desire for certain foods, beyond societal influences and its superficial limitations.

In regards to contemplating on the delights of success, do you remember a time when you felt you were doing completely what God wanted you to do? Is there a feeling in your heart that goes with this awareness? Share this bliss with someone you can trust or write about it in your journal. You can also ask to experience more of this bliss in the future.

The Purpose of Life

The purpose of life is learning how to metaphorically make lemons into lemonade while maintaining a loving, grateful heart. Growth brings more knowledge about the art of turning stumbling blocks of life into stepping stones. This growth and its resulting knowledge can lead you to connect with your personal mission for this lifetime. It's simply heaven on earth when you can vitalize your purpose for being here with joyful, productive living while turning your dreams into reality.

Remember life is either repeating itself (in cycles of feedback loops) or renewing itself (by taking you to newer, higher levels in realizing your mission in life and making your dreams come true). The choice is always ultimately yours.

Designing a New Purpose Focused for the Future

When designing a new purpose statement, try to incorporate what you received in your dreams of the future. We'll also focus on using projection. The type of projection I'm speaking about here is *not* how many people interpret projection (which is guessing what another person may be thinking or the motive behind their actions). Instead let's explore a more positive interpretation of the term *projection*.

You can use the practice of *instant projection* (reaching a higher state of consciousness while projecting yourself into future possibilities) when you combine your new purpose statement with a deepened understanding of and a proficiency with the techniques outlined in this chapter. By honing in on your new purpose and using your creative imagination, you can invite your Higher Power and the spiritual forces of the universe to enhance your future in a positive way.

Soul Is in Control

At this point you know that Soul is *in control* in phenomenal ways. It's what you've always wanted. You're in control of being responsible for getting more answers and more awareness. You, as Soul, were in control when cleaning the negative programming out your mind. It took discipline and constant testing, yet it was a labor of love filled with excitement and joy. Every day you choose to connect with Soul being in control, you grow freer.

Techniques to Give You Experiences of the Heart

Many only dream of the techniques outlined in this book. Some merely read about them without understanding or experiencing them. However, to know a thing with your heart, mind and body, you need to experience it with your whole self on a cellular level (which is the key to its success).

It also takes effort to remember to continue to surrender to your Higher Power, one step at a time. It takes a day-to-day evolving consciousness to stay open to awareness, to have the flexibility to make attitude shifts, as life reveals new adventures beyond your current success.

The greatest adventure is just beginning. This can be a spiritually golden time for discovering your true purpose, potential, and mission in life—if you so choose.

Putting It All Together: The Ongoing Journey beyond the New You

Once you've chosen a new purpose, you can adapt the techniques in this book toward the new goals you want to achieve. Any exercise, visualization or technique in this book can be modified so that you can use it over and over again.

Pick up this book and start reading with a new purpose in mind. Concepts may jump out which are pertinent to your new purpose. Use colored highlighting pens to bring attention to the parts that are most meaningful to your new purpose or goals. Date the entries. Choose a different highlighting color when you reread certain sections with a different purpose or goal in mind. Keep reviewing the exercises in this book with a sense of fun and excitement.

You're writing the story of your adventures beyond weight balance success now. It's all up to you. Right now is a great time to start making your dreams come true by making your life a conscious choice.

Chapter 12

Epilogue

When I wrote *Not Your Mother's Diet*, I distilled the harvest of my personal struggles and my patients' struggles with eating into learning adventures for others. And yet, there are those who still hunger for this truth.

Recently I took my oldest daughter shopping at the Orlando Premium Outlet Mall. As lunchtime approached, we stepped into the food court for a bite to eat. My hunger died however when I saw the selection of food from which I could choose. My daughter ordered a submarine sandwich for herself and two bottles of water, one for each of us.

I sat and looked around in amazement at all the people, their plates piled high with fast foods of all kinds. Most had sodas in their hands.

I asked my daughter, "I wonder what I could eat here?"

She said, "What about the juice place? Or there's Japanese food."

Previously I had investigated all the food selections and found none adequate for my metabolic type. I realized I'd had a similar problem at breakfast when my daughter served some carbohydrate-based treats I normally don't eat. I could have tried to make do with what was available at lunch and say nothing. However, it was time for me to speak up.

I shared with my daughter that the protein portion sizes were not sufficient and I needed nutrient-rich vegetables for sustenance. Something like baked fish, meat and steamed vegetables would help me last until supper. I explained that I felt sluggish, sleepy, and unmotivated when I ate a diet predominately based on carbohydrates. (candida grows wild with carbs.)

Later, my daughter and I shopped for groceries. We picked out a fresh fish selection and her favorite vegetable for supper. That evening we prepared a metabolically balanced meal that left both of us feeling wonderful.

Since I've personally cultivated this sensitivity, I find it a gift that I can routinely check how I feel—how my body feels—in relation to what I've eaten. This is what I teach to everyone who walks into my office. The path of weight balance freedom is simply *choosing to be conscious.*

By following *The Metabolic Typing Diet, The Food Allergy Cure, The Body" Knows" Diet* and *Not Your Mother's Diet*, bodily aches and pains, emotional irritability, anxiety, and even the depression that most people feel when eating the wrong foods can be alleviated.

Before you achieve weight balance, you'll experience dramatic positive changes in the quality of your life and freedom from mood swings and food cravings. This system of weight balance has kindled within me a deep appreciation for the process. I constantly experience a profound satisfaction with my practice as I teach these techniques and exercises to more people every day.

Everyone can experience this freedom in body, mind and spirit.

The golden key to a healthy, balanced weight you can sustain and appreciate for the rest of your life is in your hands.

Bibliography

Baer, Jean. *How to be an Assertive (Not Aggressive) Woman in Life, in Love, and on The job* (Penguin Books USA, Inc., New York, 1976).

Bradshaw, John. *Homecoming: Reclaiming and Championing Your Inner Child* (Bantam Books, New York, 1992).

Brown, Molly Young. *Growing Whole: Self Realization on an Endangered Planet* (HarperCollins, New York, 1993).

Bulfinch, Thomas. *Myths of Greece and Rome* (Penguin Books USA, Inc., New York, 1979).

Burns, David D., M..D. *The Feeling Good Handbook* (Penguin Books USA, Inc., New York, 1990).

Carson, Rachel. *Silent Spring* (Fawcett Books, Greenwich, 1962).

Cloud, Dr. Henry and Dr. John Townsend. *Boundaries: When to say Yes, When to say No to take Control of Your Life* (Zondervan Publishing House, Grand Rapids, 1992).

Ecstatic Dance. Written by Gabrielle Roth. Directed by Michelle Miller (videocassette, Sounds True, Boulder, 2000).

Food for Thought: Daily Meditations for Dieters and Overeaters (HarperCollins, New York, 1985).

Klemp, Harold. *The Book of Eck Parables; Volume 2* (Eckankar, Minneapolis, 1988).

Klemp, Harold. *The Book of Eck Parables; Volume 3* (Eckankar, Minneapolis, 1991).

Klemp, Harold. *Cloak of Consciousness* (Eckankar, Minneapolis, 1991).

Klemp, Harold. *Journey of Soul* (Eckankar, Minneapolis, 1988).

Kubler-Ross, Elisabeth. On Death and Dying (Macmillan Publishing Co., Inc., New York, 1969)

Sutherland, Caroline M. Sutherland. The Body "Knows" Diet(Sutherland Communications, Inc.Washington, 2005)

INDEX

There may be a *Not Your Mother's Diet* study group near you or you can start one yourself.

Kathleen offers you an opportunity to start you own study group using each chapter as a weekly study guide. A group can give you the ability to share with others who are interested in the principals and techniques that help you overcome your mother's diet programming. All you need is an open heart and the desire to learn. Furthermore a group can give you the support that can help you take the steps needed to succeed in your diet goals.

Please check her web site for free group guidelines to help you organize your group. http://www.notyourmothersdiet.com

Free mp3s of:

Not Your Mother's Diet - The CURE for your EATING ISSUES

I have just completed reading *Not Your Mother's Diet,* a beautifully written love gift to the reader. This is more than a diet book - for it is a workbook, journal, study guide and step-by-step approach to healing and, in the process, losing physical weight and emotional baggage. Kathleen has provided so many ways to heal that no matter what your beliefs are, many of the ways will resonate for you as the reader. She puts to rest the many myths regarding weight loss that continue to tease society into complacency and victim hood, while providing authentic clear cut actions that support personal empowerment plus healing on every level. She fills each chapter with resources for all the readers' needs including medical, nutritional, therapy, reading, intuitive awareness, and dream study.

Fuller integrates her own inspiring healing story in with practical tools that she has successfully learned and used over her many years of personal and professional work. She walks her truth. I learned so much from this book and I plan to use the knowledge, tools, and wisdom for myself and clients. I recommend it highly for all who want to heal themselves in a loving and beautiful way.

By Rev. Nancy Julian, MSW, MPH
Former Administrator of Rural Infant Care Project of Tulane Medical School
Non-Denominational Minister and Counselor

Get your free mp3s of:

Not Your Mother's Diet – The CURE for your EATING ISSUES

A $96.98 value free by going to the website: http://www,notyourmothersdiet. com and signing up on my e-mail list to receive free tips & tools for your weight/eating/body image successes.

Then go to:
http://www.kathleenfuller.net/book.mp3
Follow the instructions for downloading the mp3s.
Running time approx. 8 hours

Made in the USA